"When I come back in my next life, I'm going to look for this book. No need to bury my patterns until they are unrecognizable to myself – I'll start journaling my way to authenticity as a young person and never quit. And in the meantime, I'll be unraveling one self-defeating behavior at a time with the help of Julie Matheson's book and my own highest desires and intentions."

Stuart Horwitz, Author of <u>The Book Architecture</u> Trilogy

I was only going to write a sentence or two for each prompt, yet I was awestruck. When I finished, I had pages and pages filled with buried thoughts and missteps. The light flooded in as each layer was revealed in my notes. I am delighted to report this process works. It is powerful to say the least. Julie's voice is uniquely her own, tender but firm. This book is filled with her heart and she embraces you, the reader, as you explore the possibilities she sets forth. Her readers will hold this book close for years to come."

C. Susan Nunn, Author of <u>Song of the Earth</u> – Teacher and Editor

"This teaching is so important and is presented in such an understandable way. Our lives would be completely different if we all learned this earlier in life. It's like finding the wisdom of the ages, not unlike discovering the Dead Sea Scrolls and wishing we'd had this teaching all along."

Pam Niland, Spiritual Teacher and Student

"Julie Matheson illuminates the healing path with powerful, guided writing prompts for those who truly want to change. Her gentle presence and strong, steady support make for a constant guiding light from start to finish."

Susan Hagen, Co-author –
<u>Women Ground Zero: Stories of Courage and Compassion</u>

"This process works! I received many insights into myself and released a lot of restrictive energy that was weighing on me that I didn't even know was there. Afterward, my body felt so different – most noticeably was how open and expansive my chest felt. I had released so much energy my whole body said, 'thank you!' The shift I felt was a powerful reminder to pay more attention to all of me…my body, mind and spirit."

Debbie Dalrymple, Creator, Publisher and Editor of <u>HedraNews</u>
(A healthy living & spiritual growth newspaper.)

Lotus Flower Living®

A journaling practice for deep discovery

and lasting peace

Untangle your mind and heart once and for all

By

Julie Matheson

Lotus Flower Living®

A journaling practice for deep discovery and lasting peace

Untangle your mind and heart once and for all

This book is a product of the author's training, practice and intuition. All case studies are generalizations, not reflecting on any individual client. The content herein is designed to provide helpful, motivational and inspirational information to readers, and is not meant to be used, nor should it be used, to diagnose or treat any medical or psychological condition. For treatment of any medical or psychological problem, consult your own health professional. The author/publisher is not responsible for any specific health needs that may require medical or psychological supervision and is not liable for any damages or negative consequence from any treatment, action, application or preparation, to any person reading or following the information in this book. No warranties or guarantees are expressed or implied by the publisher's choice to include any of the content in this volume. The author/publisher shall not be liable for any physical, psychological, emotional, financial, or commercial damages, including, but not limited to, special, incidental, consequential or other damages. Readers are responsible for their own choices, actions, and results.

For more information about this title or to book a workshop, please contact the publisher:

Lotus Flower Living, LLC
1775 W. State St. #328
Boise, ID 83702
www.LotusFlowerLiving.com
Julie@LotusFlowerLiving.com

ISBN: 9781733780728

Printed in the United States of America

Cover art: Julie Matheson
Digital print of painting and cover graphics: James Krause

Receive a FREE Journal

You may download a free copy of
The Lotus Flower Living Companion Journal (.pdf) at
LotusFlowerLiving.com/Book
by validating the purchase of this book.

For my husband, Jim Matheson

For my mom, Patricia Young

And, for those who are
ready, willing and eager
to change their patterns
once and for all

Table of Contents

The Lotus Flower

So, there it is, a tiny seedling on the murky bottom of the pond.
It grows a few inches and hits a tree root.
It struggles to get its leaves loose from the root.
It grows a few more inches and gets caught in some debris.
More challenges follow.
With each struggle the plant becomes stronger,
every time growing a few more inches.
With each new set of obstacles and each new plateau,
the lotus plant develops fortitude.
One day it reaches its destination above the murky waters.
The struggle ceases.
Effort is replaced by a sense of completion.
In its achieved state of
strength, freedom and integrity,
the lotus flower opens itself to fully receive the light.
And then, in full bloom, it has
arrived, resting in peace.

Introduction: Bridging the Gaps and Taking Leaps

How I got started as a healing arts practitioner had nothing to do with waking up one day and deciding to become this. Rather, it started when I made the decision to heal my own life. Early one morning, in the mid 1980's and halfway through my undergraduate degree, I was sitting at work, sipping a cup of tea. The last few weeks had been consumed with an evening intensive codependency program. On this particular morning, my thoughts were on my challenging childhood and how life had become the way it was for me. What bothered me most about my childhood was when others didn't seem to care about the impact their behavior had on me.

I thought about all the people one person touches throughout his or her lifetime. I thought about how I want to make sure my behavior is clearheaded and respectful of others. I also pondered what it meant to be a successful person. The idea arose in me that if all I ever accomplished was to heal my own life, that my emotional health would touch every person I ever came into contact with, and this would be a worthy achievement.

As I thought about all the issues I knew I had, it occurred to me this intention to heal myself emotionally was going to require a lot of self-focus. The first block I had was that this decision sounded selfish to me. In the farming community in Ohio where I grew up, I had learned that putting one's self first in any way was considered selfish. Challenging and balancing that cultural thought-pattern was one of the first patterns I ever tackled. Eventually I concluded if I healed my own life, it would be the most unselfish gift I could ever give. I didn't know then the steadfast power of this intention, but I was on my way.

During my subsequent healing process, which spanned over twenty years until I hung out my shingle as a holistic counselor, I paid attention to what worked and what didn't work. In the early days, I would go to spiritual circles and be told that one is never fully healed and that one always has to work at it. Whenever I was in terrible emotional pain, I was told this is just the way we peel away the many layers of the emotional onion, and whenever something painful happened, it was because I had another lesson to learn.

These aren't necessarily wrong things to say but these statements made me want to find another way. Was there a way I could get out ahead of my life's lessons so life wouldn't keep hitting me over the head with another rude awakening? Was there any way to evolve my emotional life with ease and grace? And what about misperception and blind spots? Those were my biggest problems. I didn't know what I didn't know. How could I ever get out of my own way?

Thanks to my codependency studies, one of the first leaps of faith I took was embracing the philosophy that if something is bothering me about someone else's behavior, I need to find the corresponding issue within myself, change it there and then watch how my perception of the other person changes. I understood in order to change anything I had to start with myself.

Like so many healing arts practitioners of our time, I have been profoundly influenced by the philosophy that we each create our own reality through our thoughts and beliefs. When I first encountered this teaching I often couldn't sleep over feeling so excited that I had discovered the truth of reality. Although this philosophy deeply resonated with me, understanding how to work with it to manifest the experiences I wanted to have, took another leap of faith to actually grasp and apply.

Consequently, I enrolled in every course I could find that would give me a better understanding of the cause and effect nature of reality. In addition, if a teaching spoke to the mind, body, spirit connection, I was into it. I practiced affirmations, learned affirmative prayer, started meditating and began a daily journaling practice.

When I graduated with my holistic counseling certificate in 1999 the core teaching that guided my inner healing was, and still is, *the power of positive thinking* and *change your thinking – change your life*. I wholeheartedly agree with positive thinking and respect all the training I have received.

However, at that time, what was missing for me in my studies overall was an approach that helped me to bridge the gap from where I was in my belief system to where I wanted to be. I would complain about some issue in my life and be told, "Hey, don't put that out there. You don't want to create that negative reality with your words." And I'd say,

"Hey, I already did create it; chances are I will keep creating it until I figure out how to change all that is within me that keeps creating it. In the meantime, I need to talk about it as it is. I need to express my negative truth, and talk about the reality of my life, and deal with what is going on."

I mean, how many of us have tried saying positive affirmations, such as *I love myself*, only to hear a choir of deeply ingrained negative voices within us laughing back at our intentions? This was my experience. There were some areas of life where these practices worked like a champ, but for the deeper issues I needed something more comprehensive and powerful; something that helped me to discover issues and beliefs that lay beneath the surface that I didn't even know were there.

So, there I was with my shiny new practitioner's license, seeing clients for the first time, and couldn't help noticing a couple of things: first, for both my clients and me, we needed to dig deeper to discover root causes, and second, I felt the consistent urge to return to higher education to further my studies.

When I was earning my masters, focused in counseling, psychology and expressive therapies, I would share in class the philosophy that our thoughts and beliefs create our reality and no one seemed to know what the heck I was talking about. Yet, thankfully, most people seemed to understand the idea that the bumps and bruises from past experiences have a bearing on our current perception. That is, they accepted the basic building blocks of traditional psychology.

Yet, here was another gap that bothered me: the disconnect between metaphysical, spiritual concepts and traditional psychology. It became important for me to find practical ways to talk about metaphysical ideas, and to connect the sound logic of cognitive therapy to my spiritual-metaphysical understanding of reality. While it was a big leap for folks to believe that their thoughts create their reality, most could grasp the explanation that beliefs inform our thoughts, our thoughts inform our feelings and our feelings can lead to actions. Connecting the two approaches made sense to me as a building block, one to the other.

I was sorting through these frameworks and trying out different modalities in the healing arts, still wondering if I would ever truly heal my life, when I found myself blessedly immersed in practices with inner child experts and energy healers, who seemed to know how to bridge the gap between where I was emotionally and where I wanted to go. I saw in their practices a way to meet my issues right where they were, and still hold true to my vision of living free of old patterning. Life was bringing me a variety of ways to tackle my quest to heal my life.

One night before I was to see a new energy-psychology practitioner, I had a prophetic dream. I dreamt there was a tangled-up mess of string-like fibers in the center of my abdomen. In the dream, I reached an etheric hand into my stomach to grab the fibers to pull them out, yet as I tried to remove the tangled mess, it would spring right back into place. In the next scene in the dream, a practitioner helped me successfully remove the tangled mess. I knew, like one knows in vivid dreams, the tangled mess represented an emotional pattern.

The next day as I visited with this new practitioner, the dream came true – I was able to heal a tangled-up mess of an emotional pattern, effectively removing the energy of it. In that session we engaged in a process that honored exactly where I was and cleared out this negative emotional energy in a way that left me feeling extraordinarily different. It seemed when my ability to work with spiritual concepts met this practitioner's process, something magical happened. It allowed us to deal with my issue that day head-on, effectively removing it, leaving my mind completely still. I felt deeply changed. The next morning while walking my dog, I could hear a different choir of hopeful voices, of patterns beneath the one I cleared out the day before, saying, "Me, next. You can heal me next." I knew I was on to something special.

Soon, I found other holistic practitioners who also practiced this type of clearing work, and who believed you are not stuck with some pattern for the rest of your life; that you can, in fact, deeply change your patterning and move on completely. I wanted to believe this, and now I was finding others who taught practices for this. I studied with many of these clearing-work masters over the next several years, challenging the teachings and bouncing the ideas around one to the other, basking in their mastery and support, while adding my own creativity into the mix to create safer and more effective ways to do the same things.

Finally, after taking into consideration all these influences, I was able to put together a process that allowed me to clear entire patterns within myself, at once, in one sitting, leaving me feeling not just changed and different, but actually blissful. With this new approach, I would identify and then clear one pattern after another, again and again. Each time I cleared a pattern, the next one became obvious. With more layers removed, it was easier for the next one to be seen and heard. After clearing a pattern on myself I would run through the house saying, "It's done, it's done! I'll never have that issue again. I'm free!" And I would be free. In fact, others noticed I was less reactive and more peaceful.

The blissful, expanded feeling would last for days. It seemed the more peace I felt, the more peace I knew I could feel. I got good at identifying when I had a pattern that was eager to be addressed. I would work my process over and over, addressing one pattern at a time, until I was feeling more and more healed, and free. Sometimes new experiences illuminated the next issue to be addressed, and other times it was returning to an old familiar setting, like being home in Ohio over the holidays, which highlighted the right next target.

I cannot recall how long I continued this intense effort. However, I do clearly remember the day I went in to see my chiropractor, who is a gifted intuitive and channel. She shared she was seeing the energetic results of all this work and that higher guidance was remarking I had, through all my clearing-work, achieved the 'Lotus Flower.' I had no idea what that was. I wasn't looking for the *lotus flower*, per se. I had never heard of that reference, and so I asked her, "What is that?"

She explained, "It's lasting peace. It's bliss. It's an energetic placement. Your guides are saying you won't have to revisit those issues again. It's a true achievement."

This was an unexpected surprise, and a delightful gift to have a name like the *lotus flower* associated with my feelings of freedom. What's still interesting to me now as I think back to that time is I really did, for the first time in my life, feel successful. It was an intense feeling among many other joyful emotions where I felt I had arrived somewhere real. It was tangible, and for the next few months I was, very much so, in undeniable peace and bliss. Over time, this energy seemed to integrate and became my new way of being.

I do not think of this as enlightenment. Rather, it is what happened when I thoroughly addressed all the issues that bothered me most. These were self-created, issue-specific awakenings that brought fresh acceptance and freedom.

From that point on, I named my business Lotus Flower Living Holistic Counseling and I've been sharing my process ever since. At one point it was suggested to me I might create a manual to capture this process in writing, an idea that led to this book. It's like anything else – when you discover something remarkable, you just want to share it.

It is worth saying that perhaps none of the concepts in this book are new. These metaphysical concepts are age-old as are the psychological frameworks I've borrowed. What is new is how they are put together, and how I guide you to use them. What's new is the idea you can change an entire ecosystem of self-reinforcing faulty beliefs in one sitting. In fact, I encourage you to do it in one sitting so you can keep track of the depth and breadth of it and experience the pop-out-of-an-illusion feeling that happens when an entire energetic system of false beliefs moves off at once.

In this book you will find a foundational and supporting spiritual philosophy, and an explanation of how our beliefs about ourselves become self-fulfilling prophecies creating blind spots, misperceptions and repeat experiences. There is a clear, step-by-step process, in the form of 16 Discovery Prompts, each one designed to untangle, soothe and refine the most personal workings of your mind. I've also included lots of encouragement to assist and awaken the self-healer in you so you may evolve your emotional-spiritual life.

I imagine you have found this book because you have made a similar decision to the one I made that day at my desk. Something in you has said, "I want to heal my life. I want to see the world with clear perception. I don't want to wait for life to hit me over the head with my lessons through struggle. I want to evolve with ease and grace."

It does not matter what your emotional patterns are, or whether or not you are a journal keeper, or how much therapy you've tried. What matters is: are you ready? For me, I was desperate to find peace. I was desperate to stop reacting to life in ways that resulted in feeling miserable. It was a miracle to engage in a gentle process that worked every time, that allowed me to discover in one sitting all the ways my mind and heart were tangled up and confused by each issue I had.

For those who are ready, my hope is this process can safely take you where you want to go. If you want freedom and resolution on any issue, this practice is designed to help you find it. If deep, lasting peace is what you want, my hope is you can find it here, by addressing one pattern at a time. I do appreciate that it takes many leaps of faith to embrace a process like this. I hope you choose to take this leap. Then leap again and again.

Many blessings and gratitude to you for facing your inner work in order to embrace the balanced, happy, peaceful person you came here to be. I thank you, and all who love you thank you for your open mind and your willingness to change your patterns once and for all.

With gratitude and respect,

Julie Matheson

Some Initial Points

I would like to introduce you to some core concepts before we begin. While I will cover each of these in more detail in various parts of the book, to help kick-start things I am providing a quick summary here:

Behavioral and emotional patterns can be balanced and resolved by addressing the pattern in its entirety at its root cause.

The word pattern, as used in this book, is defined as a repeating thought, emotion or behavior that has occurred more than once, and which you would like to change.

When a pattern, or an issue in your life, is understood and resolved at the root cause, the emotional charge of that pattern is cleared away. This is called *clearing work*.

Beliefs become thoughts, which evoke feelings, which then translate into behavior. It all starts with beliefs.

Beliefs → Thoughts → Feelings → Behavior = Pattern

By beliefs, I mean who you think you are and how you see yourself through your own eyes.

False patterns of belief, by design, are self-deluding and self-perpetuating. Most people are not aware of the false beliefs that lie at the root of their patterns.

By writing a pattern down on paper we keep track of the breadth and depth of it. Change can happen quickly when the mind is given a chance to witness the full scope of the issue.

Clearing many patterns in this way over time may evoke the Lotus Flower signature within you, which is your soul's natural state of present-moment awareness, peace, calm and joy.

A journaling process exists for changing even the most stubborn, self-deceptive patterns. This work is called The Lotus Flower Living Journaling Practice.

Lastly, two points about co-creation:

The term co-creation (also called the spiritual law of cause and effect, or the law of attraction) pertains to our free will choice to participate with the universal creative principle of life to manifest new experiences with our thoughts and beliefs.

I capitalize words such as Life, Universe, Divine, All That Is, True Reality and Co-Creative Energy because I am using these words in place of the word God to broaden the concept of God in terms of the spiritual law of cause and effect.

How to Use This Book

To get the most from this book, I suggest you read through the entire book once from start to finish. This will give you a good understanding of the Lotus Flower Living Journaling Practice. After this, it is time to go back and dive into the Discovery Prompts focused on a single issue.

Preferably, you can set aside enough time to work through all the Discovery Prompts in one sitting so you can experience the sense of completion and freedom that follows a thorough clearing.

Addressing the entire pattern in one sitting is ideal because there is a balancing of energies that happens by doing this. If you don't have time to do all the Discovery Prompts in one sitting and must stop partway through, please be sure to keep writing until you are at least in a neutral place.

While it may be tempting to hop from issue to issue around a specific Discovery Prompt, this process works best when you address the same pattern all the way through the Discovery Prompts. This will help ensure a balanced clearing with nothing left undone.

The Lotus Flower Living Journaling Practice is designed to help you deeply understand and clear your patterns. Therefore, the writing is going to kick up stuff for you – this is good and the whole point. I hope you will dive in fully and let the Discovery Prompts work their magic for you. Please trust the process and stick with it – I will be with you on every page until your pattern has been fully addressed, cleared and released.

Admittedly, there is a lot of information for one to absorb in this book. It is my hope you will allow yourself to enter the energy of it, reading lightly and trusting what you are meant to know will stay with you. I give you permission to adopt what works for you and to leave the rest.

Thank you for committing to your personal growth. You are on your way.

PART 1: Preparing the Ground

Chapter One: The Lotus Flower

We Are the Lotus Flower

The lotus flower has long been a symbol of peace, strength, integrity and purity in Eastern cultures. The lotus flower begins its journey in a murky, muddy environment that doesn't seem nurturing to a delicate flower at all, yet it pushes against what's there, winding its way up through the obstacles, one at a time, and makes its journey to the surface anyway.

The journey of the human spirit is like this. Every obstacle serves a purpose. Every challenge, if used properly, has the potential to turn struggle into strength. It is when we don't actively push against our challenges that problems never seem to go away. Life is set up to challenge us on purpose. It's not supposed to be easy. We are meant to put effort into figuring out how to make life easier. We knew this before we came here. We knew we were meant to find peace on this planet where it seems at times to be anything but peaceful. To achieve peace in a human dimension designed for struggle is a great accomplishment for the soul.

Once we figure out how to work with life's struggles, we realize we are meant to resolve our issues and find peace with them. That is the purpose of struggle. Once our core life issues have been actively worked into a state of balance, it is like being a lotus flower in full bloom at peace emerging above the water.

Everyone has a pattern they wish they didn't have. Everyone. There isn't a soul alive who doesn't want to change something about him or herself.

Often the willingness is there but knowing how to change escapes us. Especially when it comes to deeply entrenched patterns.

The journaling practice described in this book is meant to help you overcome deeply held limiting beliefs, clearing the way for more balanced, life-affirming beliefs to take hold. The purpose is to help quicken your personal growth path and achieve lasting peace.

This is possible because journaling is an active spiritual practice. Each time we write down thoughts, we move energy. We move it from our minds to paper. We take it out of the air where it is invisible and put it onto something concrete where we can evaluate it. Talking is great. Talking moves energy, too, yet it doesn't register to the mind in the same way writing it down does. Talking can be circular, much like thought. Writing stops the circular thinking. Being willing to take this one action in itself can make a difference.

Yet we are going to do something here that takes this concept a lot further than just basic journaling can do. This book is designed to guide you to address a pattern of belief, thought, and/or behavior in yourself that changes your perception so radically, you will most likely not be able to engage in the pattern the way you did before.

Anytime anyone of us chooses to understand what makes us tick, we are rewarded with answers. Time spent putting pen to paper, as described in this book, may very well bring the answers you have sought. Of course, you want to grow. Of course, you want to understand yourself more deeply. It would be more unusual if you didn't.

Now is a good time to ask, if you could change anything about yourself – any repeating pattern of behavior, thought or emotion – what would it be?

Life on the Lotus Flower

Lotus Flower Living is a spiritual potential within each of us that becomes activated when we skillfully navigate our life's struggles through to completion. Lotus Flower Living is a state of being where one's mind is easily quiet without the typical mind chatter. It is a grounded yet expansive, easy feeling where things make more sense. This calm, alert mental-emotional state is achieved when the many moments of clarity created through a dedicated spiritual practice begin to add up, allowing us to experience life in a new, more peaceful and productive way. Lotus Flower Living is when, after digging deeply into our emotional programming, the light bulb goes on and the insights drop in, allowing us to see our issues so clearly our inherent seedlings of peace, joy, ease and grace within us blossom and take over. It's a presence and peace that give us a definite sense of having arrived somewhere wonderful.

Through this process of imagining and claiming a state of peace, joy and yes, even bliss, and working a spiritual practice, issues get resolved, right decisions get made and clear understandings allow for a new way of being and living without effort. In this allowing place, we don't feel a need to *do* this peaceful presence or to *will* ourselves to be in a balanced mind-state. Balance and clarity become the natural center point allowing us to see the beauty and purpose of our issues in their entirety, leaving us with a sense of completion. We come to understand, and even appreciate, our issues, background and challenges – not as that which defines or limits us, but that which has helped shape us. We see our struggles for what they are – something to navigate, grow and learn from.

What differentiates this journaling practice from other types of journal keeping is the sole focus on one's emotional complexion and well-being. Our emotional state drives our actions and, therefore, directly impacts our experiences. When we write honestly and fully about our emotional responses to people and events, we discover our deeper rationale. When we bring this rationale to our conscious awareness, we see more clearly how it contributes to our experiences.

When a troubling emotional pattern is entrenched in years of behavior, we can't *will* ourselves to act differently. There are simply too many conflicting beliefs fighting against the new behavior we wish to establish. We can, however, use a journaling practice that gently uncovers one belief at a time, revealing those that perpetuate the behavior.

In this writing practice, I will ask you a set of simple questions about a specific experience you had, or are having, and suggest you write down all your responses in one sitting each time you write. This practice works well because it is simple, yet comprehensive. The ways in which you currently think about your issue can undoubtedly shift because the very act of identifying the underlying beliefs gives your true soul-logic a chance to speak up, while still honoring the logic of your previous thought processes.

The Lotus Flower Living Journaling Practice, when used repeatedly, gives us the chance to experience many moments of clarity related to many different types of issues. Over time, as we have worked through our own special set of patterns, we begin to notice immediately following each writing session, the peace and joy, and at times, exhilaration, lasting longer and longer. It is then we can see how our life has truly changed.

As with any spiritual tool, this journaling practice only works if you believe in it and let it work for you. The more you use it, the more clarity you will create. One awakening leads to others, until one day you notice you no longer have to work so hard to be free of old conditioning. You are simply free.

When a spiritual tool is effective and used consistently, moments of clarity are not only possible, they become predictable. As you use this spiritual practice with an open, trusting heart, expecting to find clarity, my hope is you may find it. As you allow your writing to take you deeper and deeper, I trust you may reveal lasting peace, essentially unveiling your own soul's expression of heaven on earth.

Maybe heaven on earth isn't what you are aiming for – maybe freedom from the issues that bother you most is your primary concern. The latter was certainly the case for me. Whatever the goal, working on your own emotional health is the most unselfish choice you can make. The time you put into shifting your own perception from confusion to clarity will be a gift to yourself and everyone else whose life you touch every new day into your promising future.

My Lotus Flower Experience

When my own dedicated practice of clearing patterns with myself came to a new summit, I welcomed the change and noticed how beautifully my life had slowed down. Then, as I cleared more patterns it slowed down even more – mostly in my mind. And, not in a boring way, but in a rich, colorful, *there is so much meaning in every moment* way. I noticed life had stopped racing by. I felt as though I had caught up with life, and I could finally breathe now. It was easier to be still and find wonder in simple things. Sitting with a cup of tea in hand, just being, was enough. My typical worries stopped cycling in endless loops. It was like living in a home with organized closets. If I needed to remember a piece of information, it was easier to find it. With fewer troubles swirling front and center, I was able to count on my mind to work in the way it is meant to work, as a peaceful, skillful, ever-ready servant to my heart and purpose.

During the initial weeks of this new *lotus flower* signature, there was a presence of joy that was tangible to me, louder than any thoughts I could have about it. Joy was pulsating in my blood. Joy was my new filter through which I saw everything. When I had thoughts about patterns I wanted to clear, or ones I had already cleared, I had a whole new level of understanding that I am not these patterns. I am definitely not. I am this joy. This is who I really am. This is who we all really are.

As I had become more unified within, I appeared more unified without, and this change in vibration changed the people and circumstances I attracted. Friends and family asked me what I was doing differently. Prior to doing this work, more often than not, I had a difficult time knowing when love was real. Yet, as these new energies were anchoring within me, I somehow felt newly acceptable, loving and lovable, and in some circumstances, for the first time. The compassion I generated for myself by untangling my issues allowed me to have more compassion for others. I also became more aware of the heavy burdens my fellow humans carry around, yet with clearer boundaries about it, knowing better what is mine to do and what is theirs.

Clearing patterns allowed me to handle conflicts more skillfully by allowing me to remain centered. It enhanced my ability to be objective and better understand others' opinions and my own at the same time. I was able to see how it all fit together to form the actual reality, and not just 'my' or 'their' perception of it. Not that my mind or personality was out of a job – I was still myself. I still cared about the things I cared about. I did not feel devoid of personal challenge or lack desire for discovery or insight. In spiritual circles the ego sometimes gets a bad rap. Yet, in my new clarity, I could see that one's mind is a valuable aspect of life, and the qualities that make us each unique are not any less needed just because we took some of the edge off.

Essentially, the emotional charge that had previously caused me to exaggerate events out of proportion was substantially minimized. My worldview shifted – I could not see my circumstances the way I did before. I could not see them the same way at all. I was able to gain new insights into healthier choices and opportunities I couldn't possibly have imagined or accessed before. I forgave myself for choices and missed opportunities my misperceptions had caused, and realized I was doing the best I could. By untangling one issue at a time, I gained clarity about my own agenda and shifted the ways I give and receive with others, allowing me to more often opt for win-win solutions simply because I could finally see other, more creative options.

When I initially encountered the Lotus Flower signature, I enjoyed a period of intense joy as I recognized and appreciated the possibility of a new way of life. Over time, I became more comfortable with this new energy, and it seemed to settle in, and quiet down, yet the peaceful, joyful essence of it has never left me.

As mentioned earlier, I do not consider this experience enlightenment, but rather I see it as an emotional, spiritual achievement, which becomes possible by examining one's life, one pattern at a time, one issue at a time.

I present the process in this book as a practice that can be learned and used over and over to see things clearly for what they are, or are not. It is a peace bringer, a soother, and a resolver of issues.

In the final journaling prompt of the Lotus Flower Living Journaling Practice I will ask you to name and celebrate your new truths. For me, when I come to this part of the practice, I am often able to write truths I could not have written before I did the work. In fact, we know a pattern is successfully cleared when we can effortlessly come up with new insights we never before considered.

It is my hope your own clearing work might shift your perceptions so significantly you may come to know yourself in a new, deep and personal way. My wish is that once you reveal their roots in their entirety, previous habits and behaviors will make more sense and you can give yourself the honor and compassion you deserve. My desire is that you may create your own moments of true understanding and come face-to-face with your most authentic, precious self. With this, everything changes. It has to change, because when we change patterns at their root cause we are permanently changing our perception from the inside out. The point of power is always within us. It is right here, right now, in our grasp.

So, if you could change something, anything at all, about how you feel, behave or react in certain situations, what might it be? Ponder the possibilities as we prepare the ground for a magical first experience clearing your first pattern.

Chapter Two: Understanding Energy

Using the Negative to Attain the Positive

We all know we attract more bees with honey than with vinegar and that positive thinking will get us further in life than defeatist thinking. But what if your personal experience or reality at the moment isn't so great? Are you supposed to ignore how you feel and opt for positive thinking instead, in the hope the negative experience will go away on its own? Negative truth is negative for good reasons. Sometimes our negative experiences are the very place we need to look for answers. Often the reason an experience keeps occurring is we have not yet fully understood its deeper meaning.

If you've been influenced by New Thought Philosophy, you are likely aware of the practices of making gratitude lists, repeating affirmations and using affirmative prayer. Students of New Thought Philosophy are encouraged to keep the focus on what is going well. The idea is by focusing on what is going well, you create more of those experiences. If you have ever made gratitude lists, then you know how powerful they can be.

While it's true positive thinking is an invaluable tool for changing your mind-set, it's not as easy to do when the emotional issue you are trying to change is rooted in a matrix of deeply held beliefs that support and reinforce each other. In this case, it is the mind's tendency to argue with new beliefs that threaten the status quo. By beliefs, I am referring to how you see yourself and who you think you are through your own eyes.

Simple affirmations won't cut through a dense emotional ecosystem of negative beliefs. Sometimes when using affirmations, the issue seems to get worse before it gets better. That's because with complex issues, it is more effective to clear out the negative beliefs before you try to establish new beliefs with affirmations. Then your affirmations can work beautifully as they are meant to work.

The Lotus Flower Living Journaling Practice effectively honors your current mind-set while at the same time allowing you to plant new seeds for positive thinking. It will help you to heal what most troubles you, one issue at a time. It will allow you to create a sacred, inner sanctuary where all that you think, feel and believe will be transformed into something profoundly new and highly functional, where nothing you have ever thought or felt will be wasted. In this new state, your mind will be fertile ground for planting seeds for better experiences.

It is common to ask – *How long will this take? When will I start to feel better?* The answer is you will start to feel better fairly quickly. How long it takes has only to do with how much better you wish to feel. You can feel a little better by working a spiritual program some of the time, or you can feel really amazing if you commit to an ongoing pattern-clearing practice. You will notice you see your circumstances more clearly, improve your interactions with others, and are able to make wiser choices with each issue you bring to this practice. You will discover it is entirely possible to stimulate new awareness before a wake-up call strikes on its own.

Manifesting heaven on earth, one pattern at a time, is the goal of this book. If you know what you want to experience, and know how to work with Life to consciously co-create these experiences, then you are well on your way. But what if all this co-creative business is new to you? In the next section, we will discuss the Spiritual Law of Cause and Effect, and why the Lotus Flower Living Journaling Practice is built on this fundamental spiritual principle.

The Spiritual Law of Cause and Effect

What we believe, think, and feel has an impact on what we experience. Life honors our intentions.

What we believe is often what we create. There is a give-receive relationship between Life and us, whether we realize it or not. When it comes to understanding how Life works, it's not about judging ourselves for how we think or for what we have created. It's about appreciating how purely Life matches our intentions – energy to energy. There is only our perfect reflection coming back to us at all times, which means if we want to change the reflection, all we need to do is change the cause. What is so exciting about this understanding is the unlimited possibilities that await us. This may be a lot to comprehend and yet how wonderful is this setup in its simplicity? Nothing is random. There is a reason. There is a root cause. And sometimes that root cause traces all the way back to acknowledgment of the fact we chose to come here, where cause and effect is the spiritual law in action. Where consciously co-creating with Life is our birthright.

Another facet you may already understand is that the law of cause and effect is neutral, impersonal and works the same for everyone, just like gravity is a neutral, impersonal physical law that works the same for everyone. Life simply says, *I love you, and yes. If you believe it, it will become true for you.* Again, there is no one judging what you believe. There is only what you believe and how it manifests: cause and effect.

The law of cause and effect is sometimes presented as an abundance concept or more narrowly still as a means to attract more money. Yet this spiritual law is the very fabric of how things function across the full spectrum of life. To present it exclusively as a means for getting things might cause us to miss how wonderfully useful this spiritual law can be in helping us to fine-tune our belief system.

It is our understanding of how this spiritual law works that motivates us to use a journaling practice like this one in the first place. Once we fully understand that our beliefs are instrumental to the creation of our experiences, we naturally want to ensure our thoughts – and the beliefs that fuel those thoughts – are ones that are the truest and best for our life. How many of us honestly know what resides deep within our belief system? Sometimes the only way to know is to look for clues in our experience, and then work backwards to discover our beliefs.

While it is not true to say every thought you think creates your reality, it is accurate to say any thought fueled by emotion has the potential to create your reality. Therefore, you can change your life by changing the way you think, or, to say it more daringly, by changing the way you believe. We work at the level of the belief system because beliefs inform thought. The beliefs you have – conscious or not – influence the way you think.

According to spiritual law, wherever thought goes, matter must follow. More specifically, wherever there is a repeated pattern of thinking in a certain direction, experiences will manifest accordingly. Thank goodness Life works so simply. What makes this simple truth difficult to master is Life mirrors back to us our conscious beliefs, the ones we are aware of and can more easily identify, and our subconscious beliefs – the beliefs we hold in the deeper spaces of our consciousness. Subconscious thoughts and beliefs have just as much, or more, influence on our experiences as the beliefs we hold in our known awareness.

Discovering subconscious beliefs, then, is essential. If a certain experience keeps happening and you are baffled by what is causing it, your subconscious beliefs are the place to look.

The good news is, you can use the law of cause and effect to create any kind of wonderful life-situation you desire, as long as it doesn't infringe on someone else's right to have or be. It may be you are meant to have exactly what you picture, or maybe Life has an even better idea that is beyond your wildest dreams. The most effective intention is the one that says, *this* or something better, or whatever is the highest good for all involved. When we, with active faith, open our intention to the highest and best outcome, we move energy beyond the limited awareness of our personal ego. Then miracles happen.

Perception or Reality

Decisions we have made in response to past experiences establish many of our beliefs about ourselves. When past experience colors our perception, perception is not reality. Certain unconscious beliefs left unchallenged become repeat experiences. Repeat experiences, then, establish and reinforce beliefs. For example, let's say a child was rejected by friends in grade school and thereby made an unconscious decision he was somehow not acceptable. Now as an adult, his fear of being rejected and his belief in his unacceptability cause him to subconsciously not only expect to be rejected, but also to exhibit behaviors that ensure he will be rejected. And, so the cycle goes: previous experiences create subconscious decisions, which become beliefs, which create experiences, which reinforce the basic beliefs that drive repeat experiences, and on and on. A pattern is established.

It helps to understand how perception works. As a human, there are many filters through which you perceive your circumstances: you have a personality, an ego, an astrological chart, a programmed inner-child and inner-parent dialogue, cultural messages from your community and religion, unique health challenges and many beliefs from years of emotional imprints from every kind of personal experience. The list of filters through which we perceive our circumstances is long, varied, interconnected and synchronistic.

All of these filters influence your beliefs and, therefore, your picture of reality – *how life is for you*. When we realize that at the soul level we are none of these influences, it helps us detach from them enough to look objectively at them as they show up in our patterns. In truth, you are a strong, whole, healthy and complete spirit who is always centered in peace and connected to divine wholeness. Your behavioral patterns, as influenced by your human filters, are not the full picture.

In the Lotus Flower Living Journaling Practice, we are not going to deny your human experience, rather we are going to consider the difference between you as an eternal, invincible spirit and you as a human with many perceptive filters. These filters are all optional. You are allowed to change them. You are allowed to make new decisions about the filters through which you see the world or, better yet, to opt for the bravest choice of all: to see the world purely as it exists in fact – the good, the bad, the beautiful and the ugly.

Chapter Three: The Basics of Clearing Work

What is Clearing Work?

When a pattern is changed at root cause, the emotional charge of that pattern is cleared away. This is called clearing work. Another common term is energy work. It is possible to permanently clear the charge of an entire pattern in one sitting. While it is true some patterns run deep and may require more than one attempt to fully harmonize the issue, this method allows you to remove many layers at once, giving you significant relief. Each set of layers you remove reveals more clues about how to go deeper next time.

While you can expect certain core themes to repeat with continual use of this practice, this doesn't mean you didn't successfully clear the pattern. If you wrote out your pattern on paper using this journaling process and felt a shift resulting in a new perspective your mind can no longer argue with, then you did actually clear it successfully. When previously addressed themes reappear, it is safe to assume there is an overlap with another pattern at play. Just know it will be much easier to clear that pattern because you will already know many of its strategies. Once the key to one pattern is found, it opens the doorway to other patterns. Inevitably, then, liberation becomes possible.

Take a moment now to jot down 5 – 10 things that are bothering you. From this we will identify a pattern for you to address.

What is a Pattern?

As we now understand, by the time most problems reach our awareness as a serious issue, they have become a repeat pattern of behavior or experience. In the context of this clearing work, a good working definition of a *pattern* is a set of painful, frustrating behaviors, feelings or experiences that have repeated more than once, and which you resist happening again. It can feel like a force of energy that takes over, seeming to have a life of its own through you, resulting in feelings of shame and regret. It might cause you to look around for someone else to blame. It might leave you in a state of confusion wondering what just happened, not knowing how to prevent it from happening again, and dreading that it will happen again.

If a negative experience has happened three or more times and the common denominator is you were there when it happened, then it is safe to conclude it is your pattern. You own it in some way. And since you own it, you can change it. You have the power, and now you will have the tools.

Exaggerated Reactions and Where They Come From

As you think about a negative pattern you'd like to clear, have you ever felt that your pattern seems bigger than just you? As if every painful pattern in the world lives in you, and you can't possibly ever surmount it? The reason for this is because some of our more troubling patterns connect us to the greater collective, unconscious energy of pain and suffering.

Every kind of pain and suffering that has ever happened on earth throughout all time has left an imprint, a memory, in the collective, subjective mind of humanity. Other terms you may be familiar with are *pain-body*, *race-suggestion*, the *collective unconscious*, or *collective-subjective-thought*, to name a few.

In other words, all thoughts and actions in this particular realm of the human race remain a part of the whole, creating a collective field of lower vibrational ideas that connect to our subconscious mind through our patterning, influencing our thoughts. This influence often sounds like gross generalizations and causes us to use words like *always, never, everyone* and *no one*. It fuels stereotypical thinking.

By clearing patterns, you disconnect yourself from this weighted, collective, pain-sourced energy, which is why clearing patterns can be so liberating. Literally you will be shutting the door that allows pain to enter through your particular patterning.

You Are Not Your Patterns

One way to foster objectivity and to disconnect from the collective, unconscious pain-energy is to realize you are *not* your patterns. Patterns are just patterns. They are not you. This also means you are not your thoughts, and you are not your behaviors. You are more than these things. You are an eternal being living an earthly experience where human patterning is involved. One of our primary reasons for coming to this planet at this time is to set things straight for ourselves on this fact: We wanted the challenge of trying to remember who we are in a place where remembering the bigger picture is difficult. We are just reminding ourselves. This is a place where we can push against obstacles to gain consciousness.

It is time then to be aware of what is influencing the ways you believe that are distracting you from the beautiful spirit you are. To lovingly observe yourself while you clear a pattern, you will need a detached, objective mindset. By understanding you are not your patterns, you give yourself the necessary objectivity and perspective needed for this practice.

Every time we clear out a faulty belief pattern, more of *who we are* and less of *who we are not* will be running the show, which means we can now function with greater soul-presence. More soul-presence makes it easier for us to make better choices. Our own beloved soul would never allow us to hurt or betray ourselves. When hurt and self-betrayal express themselves through our patterns, it's because we have become disconnected from who we truly are – beings with balanced power and true spiritual discernment.

How Beliefs Become Patterns

So, here's how it happens: We have beliefs that became established when we were children that tell us *this is how life is.* These beliefs inform our thinking. When we experience something new, we generate thoughts about it. Then we have an emotional response to our thoughts. Thoughts show up in the body as feelings. Feelings then lead to action. So, it goes like this:

Beliefs → Thoughts → Feelings → Behavior = Pattern

If you don't yet know what you believe within the context of your pattern, then just work backwards:

>What was your reaction? How did you behave?

>What was your feeling that caused your behavior?

>What were you thinking that caused your feelings before, during and after you took action?

There you go. Now you have clues to your beliefs. We will repeatedly use this basic exercise as we write out each of your patterns. Eventually you will ask yourself – What do I believe about this situation and my relationship to it? Then you will evaluate – Are these beliefs true? For now, understanding that beliefs become thoughts, which evoke feelings, which then translate into behavior, is key.

Are any patterns coming to mind you would like to clear? When choosing a first pattern to work on, answer the question – *What bothers you the most?* What issue occupies your mind more than any other right now? Not the one you think you should work on, rather the one that is tormenting you at this moment. From your list of 5 – 10 bothersome things, which item stands out? Has something similar ever happened before? If so, there's your pattern. That's the place to start.

Chapter Four: A Healthy Reference Point Guides the Way

A New Reference Point for Healthy Behavior: When painful behavioral patterns first get established it doesn't take long for these patterns to feel so familiar that we forget what healthy behavior originally felt like. After a while, imbalance feels normal. When unhealthy behavior feels normal and healthy behavior feels abnormal, it can feel as though your feet are not securely on the ground.

The key is to establish a new reference point for what balance feels like. If we are going to clear your pattern, you will need to have a healthy, balanced reference point to guide the way. Otherwise you will journal in circles, not knowing where you are going.

This new reference point is your own wholeness. I'm going to ask you to find and connect to your own natural, peaceful state of being. We all have this. No matter what is going on, we all have a place at our center that remains untouched by circumstances. It's the place where you go when you need a moment of truth.

This is where a little faith comes in. When it comes to your spirit, there is always a place at your center that is connected to a power greater than you that is immediate, stable and ready to be used for good. This stable, honest, loving presence is your core reference point in this clearing work.

Going a step further, and getting back to our co-creation principles discussed previously, we choose to have a spiritual perspective trusting there is a loving, stable power and presence that permeates all of life, which is immediately available for our own use. Not only is it in each of us, it is all around us, regardless of any appearance to the contrary.

Each time we choose to focus on our wholeness we rise above our patterning and can see solutions that move us beyond struggle. When we switch out of the appearance of struggle and move into the flow of solution-based behavior, healthy behavior feels normal again. Seeing truth beyond appearances with your feet securely on the ground is what it's all about.

Beliefs → Thoughts → Feelings → Behavior

Our Beliefs are the Root of Heaven or Hell for Us: Again, by beliefs, I mean how you see yourself and who you think you are through your own eyes. Our beliefs get established through repeat experiences, both good and bad, and by the way we interpret our experiences. Nine different people with nine different personality types will potentially have nine different viewpoints about a single incident. That's why it's important to know your own filters. Your filters influence what you see and they influence the beliefs you establish as true. We are each responsible for knowing our filters and how they inform what we perceive. When it comes to what we experience, our beliefs start the whole chain reaction from perception to creation, from thought to behavior.

Negative experiences establish negative belief patterns, and what we don't clear out or heal, we will repeat. We can count on it. Let's consider the idea about how we interpret everything through past experience. Again, most all of our decisions about who we are as people get decided when we are kids, and then these decisions become *the way life is* for us.

For example, you might say, I'm an introvert or an extrovert. I'm stubborn. I'm smart. I'm stupid. I excel at art. I'm an athlete. I'm clumsy. I'm beautiful. I'm ugly. I'm daring or I'm careful. People like me. People don't like me. I can't do anything right, or I'm a superstar. These decisions and even more intricate decisions than these get established as beliefs and these beliefs then become our self-fulfilling prophecies.

As children, we made thousands of decisions that became beliefs, and these decisions then dropped into our subconscious minds so we could live on automatic pilot and not have to reinvent ourselves in each moment.

Having beliefs reoccur is mostly helpful. What isn't so great about this is that not all of these decisions are based on truth. If a decision was made based on a painful experience that occurred when we were too young to fully understand it, chances are we made a false assumption about ourselves based on this false analysis. And, because this decision was rooted in actual experience, it was very convincing. To our emotional and physical body, it feels like fact. Since beliefs rooted in experience tend to repeat themselves in future experiences, the belief – true or not – gets reinforced. The groove gets deeper. The cycle continues. It's no wonder change can be so difficult.

When it comes to beliefs being continuously reinforced through repeat experiences, what happened in the past doesn't stay in the past. Beliefs from past experience cause us to misinterpret current circumstances. Misinterpreted circumstances cause us to reinvent the beliefs as seen in our mind and as felt in our body. This gives a whole new meaning to *consciousness* and *free will*. (*Consciousness*, meaning the level of our awareness. *Free will*, meaning our own volition.) When past experience is the lens we are looking through, it's difficult to perceive today's events clearly and to feel as though we have any control over those events. We do though. We have a lot more control and free will than we realize.

Beliefs → Thoughts → Feelings → Behavior

Cause and Effect and Free Will: When it comes to clearing out limiting belief patterns, understanding **cause** (beliefs and thoughts) and **effect** (feelings and behaviors) helps us redefine what is meant by free will. Since the beliefs we hold in our conscious and subconscious minds act as a lens we see the world through, reinventing themselves as self-fulfilling prophecy, our free will isn't just what we know we believe and think about. It also includes the buried beliefs we accumulated long ago that we no longer consciously remember. Sometimes we don't know what we believe about certain issues until we try to manifest something new. Then those buried, limiting beliefs come to the surface reminding us they are still there, discouraging us from establishing new behaviors. In the Lotus Flower Living Journaling Practice, we bring old limiting beliefs to the forefront on purpose with the intent to clear them out. And, why not? It's possible. We absolutely can.

Now, let's move on to the nitty-gritty of how limiting beliefs get established.

Chapter Five: Beliefs

How Negative Beliefs Are Learned: When a shocking experience causes us to encode limiting beliefs about ourselves, the beliefs themselves are so painful we automatically come up with ways to compensate for the beliefs we coded. No one wants to feel pain, and so we instinctively try to resist these painful beliefs because they hurt. It may seem insane that we would harbor beliefs we resist, and yet this is exactly what happens when energy from shocking experiences gets trapped in our emotional body. It makes sense then, when we give voice to those beliefs, we open the doorway that lets that energy out. In doing this, we give that trapped, dense energy a chance to give us the message it was trying to deliver in the first place. We needed that information when we first had the experience to help make proper sense of the situation. We need the same information now to clear out our pattern and the false beliefs that propel it.

As an example, let's say at age two an adult handed you a sparkler on the 4th of July. You were mesmerized by it, staring at it with awe and wonder. You were in peaceful, openhearted amazement as you held this magical wand. Then imagine out of nowhere an adult gets alarmed that someone just handed a two-year-old a sparkler. He or she freaks out causing a big scene. The frantic adult yanks the sparkler out of your hand and screams at you in front of everyone. You have no idea what you did wrong. One moment you are staring at a magic stick in wonderment. The next you are being humiliated in front of a crowd of people. That's shock.

Something just happened you don't understand. Next, you either cry or suppress your feelings or both. Perhaps no comforting words are offered to help you make sense of all this. After all, all the onlookers are just as shocked as you are. You have no idea what you did to cause that reaction. Your mind then immediately starts generating thoughts and ideas about what happened, trying to figure it out. You are two years old, so your logic about why this happened gets recorded at the mental level of a two-year-old.

When something shocking happens, a new decision about ourselves can be encoded impressively fast and remarkably deep. That we are able to do this so quickly and permanently is evidence of how easy it is to learn a new belief – at least when emotion is involved. When shock is involved, you have adrenaline. When adrenaline is involved, you have fear. Fear creates and fuels negative beliefs. That's why we don't usually encode positive beliefs when shocking events occur.

Beliefs → Thoughts → Feelings → Behavior

So, let's talk a bit more about how shock and trauma influence our beliefs, and our overall related rationale, by considering our age at the time the beliefs got established.

Emotional Age Determines Belief Logic: Think for a moment about all the shocking things that happen to a person from birth to age twenty-five. The possibilities are endless. Now, try to recall yourself at various ages and think about your emotional logic at each age. Your emotional logic evolved as you evolved, depending on many factors: your family and culture, your personality, your aptitude, and your experiences, etc. The way you encode beliefs – the details, the logic, and the emotional maturity – is determined by the age you were at the time the event happened.

Ever see a person in their sixties throw a tantrum and think to yourself he or she is acting like a two-year-old? That's likely because something just triggered an unconscious memory of a shocking event that happened when he or she *was two years old*. When it comes to emotional shock and trauma, the past doesn't stay in the past, until we address it.

Beliefs → Thoughts → Feelings → Behavior

Detach and Observe While You Feel: There are many mental, emotional and physical processes going on at once when a negative belief gets embedded, and often there are many nuanced and sometimes conflicting beliefs that get established at one time. Considering some of the beliefs are themselves nuanced and complex, we need a process to release them that is equally potent.

Therefore, I'm going to ask you to do several things at once while you address your pattern in this writing practice. I'm going to ask you to detach from the story of the pattern enough so you can observe it objectively and try to not be too identified with it as being who you are. At the same time, I'm going to ask you to be identified with it enough so you can still sense the messages of the pattern. Since your mind is smart enough to encode many beliefs at once during a single incident, it's also true your mind can hold several ideas at once while you decode a pattern. The Lotus Flower Living Journaling Practice is designed with this very concept at its core.

I will never ask you to call your experience untrue. We won't argue with your experience at all. I will, however, ask you to allow your soul-logic to help you separate the story that was coded from the facts of what happened. I will ask you to observe the thinking and logic at the level of the pattern, not at the level of your conscious mind, keeping in mind the beliefs which were established in childhood will be at the age level you were at the time.

Some of the beliefs may sound rather ridiculous to you as you revisit them. I've had clients tell me they don't feel comfortable admitting some of the messages of their patterns for this reason. I'm preparing you in advance – this is a normal reaction.

You might choose to be entertained by what you discover in your patterns. From an adult perspective, many of the messages you will identify might sound rather funny. Some will be sad, others pathetic. This is all to be expected. Yet from your detached, objective position, you won't judge them. You will simply write them down as you flow through the steps of this practice.

Chapter Six: Thoughts and Feelings

Connecting Thoughts to Experience: We live in a human reality of cause and effect, so we can expect there to be a relationship going on between what we think and what we create in our experiences. In this journaling practice we begin by observing the experiences we have created. Can you name a time when you know you created your own experience? That is, can you connect thoughts, desires, wishes or fears to events that occurred in your life? A desire came true and you know it came true because you asked for it to come true? You desired it and it happened, or you feared it and it happened? The relationship we have with Life might seem like magic, but this is just the way Life operates when it comes to cause and effect. Life responds to the ways we think and believe. This is simply how it works.

On a more concrete level, our feelings inform behavior and our behavior greatly influences how other people respond to us. If we want to change the way others respond to us, we need to change our behavior. But before we can do that, we need to identify the behaviors we have that aren't working. It gets a little tricky when we are too close to our own behavior to realize when it isn't working. It requires us to take a leap from it's something out there making me miserable to it's me in here making me miserable: it's my behavior that is affecting my experience and this is something I can actually change.

Beliefs → Thoughts → Feelings → Behavior

Thoughts Become Feelings: Thoughts are generated by your mind, whereas feelings are the effect of thoughts felt in your body. If you want to change the way you feel, you must first change the way you think.

Again, if you are not sure what you think, tune into your feelings and work backwards: I am feeling _____ , therefore, the thought that is causing this feeling is _____.

What are you feeling right now? By now it is probably obvious that the ability to identify and name specific feelings is essential for this process. Many people are not able to identify their feelings, let alone the thoughts and logic that cause them. We cannot communicate with anyone in a real and honest manner if we are not in touch with our deepest levels of belief and logic. Tangled strands of logic lead to mixed messages we inadvertently send to others and to Life. It just makes good sense that we can only be as honest as our deepest levels of reasoning allow us to be.

We identify feelings by stopping in the moment and asking – *What am I feeling right now?* A feeling is usually one word: mad, sad, glad, afraid or some derivative of these. If you must use a full sentence to name a feeling, it's not a feeling, it's a thought. A thought comes from your mind, whereas a feeling is felt in your body. Battles in the mind can be fought and won in seconds by taking a moment to nail down a core feeling. When a feeling is properly identified and fully felt, it moves through you like water, leaving only the information it is meant to deliver. When feelings are ignored, they will keep repeating until you stop to register their message, like a squeaky door that continues to squeak until you oil it. You might think it is too time consuming to listen to your feelings, but it's so much more time consuming and draining to be bombarded by the same feelings over and over that never get addressed, similar to living in a house with too many loud, squeaky doors.

Beliefs → Thoughts → Feelings → Behavior

I Feel It Therefore It's Mine: Another leap we need to make is the conclusion that our feelings are never caused by someone else.

Considering our feelings are generated by how we choose to think, and how we choose to think is determined by our personal belief filters, we self-generate all of our own feelings. Therefore, it is never a true statement to say – *You made me feel* _____.

In the Lotus Flower Living Journaling Practice, we own all of our own feelings otherwise this practice won't work very well. In working this process, it becomes clear that the more you can acknowledge your own experience and take ownership of your own self-generated feelings, the more negative patterns you can clear out and the faster you can transform your life. In fact, the moment you fall prey to pointing a finger at someone else, all power is lost. If you want the *lotus flower* – and I'm telling you, you do want it because it's heaven on earth – then you'll need to understand and appreciate what you bring to the table.

There comes a time, maybe in a therapist's office, at a 12-step meeting, or with a close friend, when it finally gets pounded into one's mind that it's time to stop focusing on what he, she or they did or didn't do. It is time to stop talking about the problem at the level where you have no power to change it. When this happens, a profound shift is made. The light bulb goes on. You begin to realize life isn't happening to you. No one is against you. No one is out to get you. Things happen, and you are responsible for how you choose to interpret them. It becomes apparent that until you can keep the focus entirely on what you bring to the situation, you are not going to get anything accomplished. Sustained obsession on other people's behavior where you do not have any control only encourages the pain cycle. Therefore, you might adopt this frame of mind –

No one makes me feel anything. All my feelings are self-generated. Every feeling I feel is generated by my own thinking and belief system, as created by my own experiences.

In our home we avoid saying – *You made me feel _____*, because it is never true. Even as someone who is empathic to others' feelings and who has to work diligently to discern my own feelings from what I sense around me, I refuse to blame others for how I feel. I might say – *When you do such and such, I tend to feel this way about it*, but I am clear that the reaction is mine. It's an important distinction and boundary to claim.

Therefore, the first power-move we make in this practice is the decision to own our feelings, which means owning our own experience.

If I am having an exaggerated reaction to some situation, especially if it is not the first time I've had a similar reaction, then I probably have a pattern worth investigating. If I'm feeling it, it's mine.

But don't worry, you won't have to feel these feelings for long, because we are going to do something about them. Identifying our feelings is how we listen to ourselves. It's how we keep our focus earth-based, reality-based and body-based. When we get in the habit of identifying feelings felt in the body, we discover something: the body remembers!

Chapter Seven: The Body Remembers

Body Memory: What the body can't assimilate, it can't eliminate. This is true on more levels than just common sense for good digestive health. When it comes to painful memories held in the body, especially events that took you by surprise, the emotional body, which is inseparable from the physical body, can become jammed with too much emotional energy at once. When too much emotional energy comes at us too quickly, and when we don't have enough time or skill to make sense of a painful experience, that emotional energy gets tied up in the body.

Since this is true, when a painful memory gets triggered, the body's instinctual fight-or-flight response gets activated. It doesn't matter how long ago the event happened. To the body, when an old, emotional wound gets triggered, it is as if it is happening right now. The fight-or-flight response is evidence that the body always remembers what happens to us emotionally. This is often what causes us to overreact or to be overly cautious on certain decisions. This is why we sometimes have spontaneous, inexplicable reactions to certain events.

With pattern clearing, one of the goals is to change your body's automatic fight-or-flight reaction (resulting from certain stimuli) to one of an objective, neutral *I have other options here* kind of response. It is maddening to act in ways that betray your own spirit. It's unhealthy to react in ways that betray your body. As we better understand why we have reacted in certain ways in the past and as we change those automatic reactions at the body level, we change our cellular memory going forward. When you change your mind, you change your body.

Beliefs → Thoughts → Feelings → Behavior

Body Memory is Crucial to Our Clearing Work: Painful memories held in the body as a physical response to a painful event will repeat over and over again until you clear them out. It's important to note, each event, of the string of events these stored memories recreate, will *feel* the same. However, these repeat events may not *look* exactly the same. We will discuss this point more later.

The fact that traumatic and shocking experiences reinvent themselves is not a mystical phenomenon. This is simply nature at work trying to keep you safe, reminding you of the past so you can learn and be smarter the next time. Yet, because messages recorded during a time of fear are not the full story, this is not helpful. It can be misleading. The charge of these stored memories needs to be cleared out so you can see current events as they are occurring now, not as filtered imprints through the lens of past, painful experiences.

Beliefs → Thoughts → Feelings → Behavior

Limiting Beliefs Affect Our Physical Health: What we think, feel, and believe in the form of knotted, unprocessed body memories can show up as disease in the body. This is why stress is hard on your health. When a thought, reinforced through experience held in the body as repeat feelings, grinds a deeper groove, the body has to compensate for the imbalance this creates. Again, there is nothing extraordinary about this idea. This is just common sense. We can ignore this cause and effect relationship between our thoughts and our body, but why would we? Clues from the body are often the most obvious and the most trustworthy. We would only ignore these clues if we had not yet made the connection between our thoughts and our bodies. So now we can add another component to our equation:

Beliefs → Thoughts → Feelings → Behavior/*Health*

Chapter Eight: Conscious Co-Creation with Life

Affirmative Prayer and Intention Setting

In this journaling practice we begin with the end in mind. Both *affirmative prayer* and *intention setting* are ways of aiming your mind toward the results you wish to achieve. Affirmative prayer is similar to that of stating an affirmation but it goes a few steps further, and connects us to something deeper. An affirmation, first of all, is a positive, present tense 'I' statement that names what you want as though you already have it. For example: I am healthy. I am happy. I am peaceful. I love my life.

Given the definition of an affirmation, an affirmative prayer then is the act of unifying with the co-creative principle of life, saying many related affirmations together to create a mental-emotional state that causes you to vibrate at the same level and frequency as the condition you wish to manifest. When we pray affirmatively, we are claiming the condition we want to experience as though it already exists. We aren't begging Life to answer our prayer, rather we are acknowledging that what we want to experience already exists in the All-Possible and by claiming it for ourselves, we co-create it for ourselves. Instead of hoping by chance some wonderful experience finds us or hoping some divine power takes pity on us and gives us what we desire, with affirmative prayer we recognize we are part of the Divine. Divine power exists in us, through us and around us. In this, we realize that we are active participants in an abundant universe where anything is possible, and all we need to do is claim it!

With affirmative prayer we create an energetic connection to All That Is. You might call this God, Goddess, Oneness or Divine Source. I often use the words Life or Universe to talk about this all-inclusive presence. This co-creative network responds to our beliefs. This power and presence is what makes prayer possible. It is also the same energy network that allows us to think of someone just before they call us or to know when a loved one is in danger.

This co-creative network does not judge us by how we use it. It is impartial whether we use it to manifest worries, or to create a million dollars, or to find the love of our life, or to heal a deep emotional wound. It is neutral, unbiased and is consistently *on*. It works, and always has, whether we are aware of it or not.

Whatever you most desire right now already exists in the All-Possible. So, it's really a matter of knowing what you want, trusting you can have it, and receiving it once it shows up. There isn't any one right way to pray, and it doesn't even matter what you call it exactly. Call it focused intention. Call it getting clear on what you really want. Call it positive thinking. Honestly, isn't that what faith is all about? Imagining something as already real?

Our desires call to us as much as we call to them. The fact we desire something in the first place is evidence it is possible to have it, otherwise we wouldn't have thought of it. When we pray affirmatively, we literally tap into True Reality, making contact with the frequency of the higher good we wish to experience. Once we have nailed the feeling, affirmative prayer is the act of giving the Divine the go-ahead. Essentially, we say – *Yes, Universe, I claim this or something better*. Boom! That's it. The feeling was captured and the claim was made. That's an affirmative prayer.

If any fear or doubt is felt during this process, we can do some clearing work on what surfaced, and do the prayer again. The more we can connect with the true unlimited potential that exists for us, while remaining in a neutral, open-minded state, the easier it is to connect to the desire that is also trying to find us. Sometimes we need to say a prayer just to get clear on what we want to create.

The point is to allow what you can't yet see to be real for you, real enough so you can anchor the feeling of that desire. Grasping these concepts is necessary as we dig into this clearing process, particularly the aspect of neutrality. A neutral, open mind-set makes it easier to hold several concepts in your awareness at once.

It is okay to admit when you don't like something about your current experience and, at the same time, acknowledge that having what you do want exists in the All-Possible. Our heart spaces are where these two worlds can meet without conflict. In the heart space, it can all be true at once without contradiction. You have likely felt the sensation of a really good co-creative moment, one that turns out to be effective, drop into your gut at the let-go moment. That satisfying feeling lets you know you connected to the right energy in your heart center. Once you have felt a satisfying connection, you say *yes* and send it out there.

Co-creative energy is given maximum license to work in our favor when we trust Life to deliver a result better than we imagined. The trick is to not dictate how our desires will manifest. Sometimes affirmative prayer is made too complicated by trying to control what we think is the best solution. We try to imagine how it will all unfold, and then put restrictive guidelines into our prayer, when in fact, all we need is pure intention fueled by pure emotion. Life will take care of the details of how, what and where. When the emotion is pure and balanced, we can just trust and forget about it.

If you have ever made floating bubbles with a bubble-wand and soap, you know the bubble won't float unless you create and release a complete bubble. If you don't slice the wand through the air and fully release the bubble from the wand, the bubble will collapse and the soap will drip off your wand. Effective prayers are like the strong soapy bubbles that leave your wand and float away. That's the sensation we want when we release our intentions. Wherever that bubble goes and whatever it does, is fine. We can trust it because our intention was pure. The effect will be good because the cause was true.

Connecting Intention to Results

It is a natural tendency to want to evaluate our impact on our surroundings. Conscious people want to improve and upgrade how they affect their own experiences, and care about their impact on other people. Connecting intention to results is a skill we use to observe our patterns in action.

In this work, it is necessary to be able to name examples where you can connect thought (cause) to experience (effect), where something happens and you acknowledge to yourself –

I recognize my part in creating that and I can identify what I was thinking and believing which played a role in creating my experience. I am responsible for all I think, say and do. I am accountable for everything I co-create. I know the task is mine when it comes to evaluating how my experiences turn out and for making corrections based on what I learn.

Taking note of how events turn out is not self-blame, by the way. This is merely observing cause and effect at the level of thought and belief. Adding blame distorts the point. It would be like judging gravity as bad or blaming yourself for the effect of gravity. Sure, if you misuse gravity and jump off a cliff expecting to fly, then you would need to be clear that it was your misuse – and judgment about the misuse – that fed the feeling of blame. You might choose to walk away from the bottom of the cliff, saying – *Wow, that was a good learning experience, I won't do that again.* (Or, maybe you'd need to learn this in the next life because now you are dead!)

You are always free to investigate why circumstances turn out the way they do. It's great to learn why. Once you know why, you will look back over your scribbled notes thinking, no wonder I behaved that way, considering the beliefs that were feeding my pattern. Seeing it all laid out in one place makes self-forgiveness easier, and then you can let it go.

Honesty Will Get You There

The more honest and sincere you are, the more you will gain from this practice. Have you ever had someone offer you an apology and then proceed to make a million excuses for why they did what they did? It can leave you feeling as though you received no apology at all. Compare this against a clean apology such as – *I'm so sorry. I see my mistake and I am truly sorry.* Period. It's a clean apology; it hasn't been so cluttered up with excuses that you can't find the actual apology. These are words you can feel and believe.

If you have the humility needed to offer a clean apology, then you have the ability to effectively clear a pattern. If you don't have this ability, you might wish to address it as a pattern. It could be the perfect place to start.

The Emotional Body and Intentions

You might think of the emotional body as a cloud of energy that surrounds and permeates your body. Your thoughts and feelings influence the quality, density and vibration of your emotional body. The emotional body influences your physical body. This is why negative, dense emotional energy can cause serious damage to your physical body if you don't clear it out.

We care about the emotional body, because emotions felt in the body have more ability to create our experiences than thoughts do. One of the reasons we care about thoughts is because they fuel emotion. Emotion is the fire that fuels our intentions. We can think positively all day long, but until it registers at the body level, we won't move energy that way. If you want to move positive energy in your life, you'll want to practice feeling positive emotions in your body. Imagining a desired experience, and feeling it as though it already exists, moves energy through your body and out into your experience. If you believe it, your body will believe it. No one refutes the power of the placebo effect.

When it comes to the power of focused intention-setting for this work, I will ask you to reference your body and to access the information held in your emotional body.

Your Intention Guides Your Process

The intention you have at the onset will not only set the tone for your clearing work, it will guide you and keep you on track the whole way through the Discovery Prompts. It will give you a reference point with which you can then compare the lower frequency of energy you will be clearing out. Since you will be referencing your primary intention during the entire clearing process, the intention needs to be crystal clear to you; so clear you can name this is what isn't working well and this is what I want instead. For example, you might say – *If and when _____ area of my life is working really well, it will feel like _____ .*

It's necessary to feel the essence of your intention in its purest form because the energy that drops in after you have cleared your pattern will be the energetic essence you created when you stated your intention. The new energy will carry the wisdom you were disconnected from when the old pattern first became established. That's why you can be assured of not repeating the same limiting behavior again. You literally will have new reference points of wisdom within you informing your thoughts going forward, and you will trust them.

Chapter Nine: The Blessed Struggle

Struggle Exists for Good Reasons

Without struggle and without painful events, no one on earth would have any compassion, wisdom, emotional depth or perspective. We would not be able to empathize with one another, and, therefore, would not be able to bond. As long as the struggles we face don't cause us to completely shut down, they give us reason to search our souls for answers, bringing us closer to our true selves.

The whole point of coming to a human existence designed for struggle is to learn how to *not* struggle *with* the struggle. Said another way, we are here to be conscious. We came here to grow for our own soul's sake. Choosing not to struggle in a physical dimension designed for struggle is how we satisfy our soul's aspiration. It's our aim, then, to figure out what *not struggling* means individually for each of us. It's our task to overcome our struggles in a way that allows us to sincerely choose ease and flow instead. As in –

I'm really choosing to figure out what this means for my life and I'm choosing to do it full on. I'm choosing to get to a place where I don't have to think about it anymore. I'm not trying hard to not struggle, because that's still struggle. I choose to evolve and to flow.

Your Struggles are Finite

Everyone has patterns they need to address. No one is sitting on the sidelines problem-free. Yet we each have a unique set of struggles. Have you ever noticed other people have a different set of issues than you have? That's because we don't have to solve all the world's problems within ourselves. We only have to deal with our own special set of issues. Your issues are somewhat finite and once you have dealt with your own special set of issues, you find yourself living your own version of heaven on earth.

Given this viewpoint, heaven on earth seems achievable. It's not that all your problems magically disappear. The way you think about them evolves, letting you see things for what they are. Your patterns no longer seem to have agendas of their own distorting all the facts. You might think of it as liberation, or freedom. You might simply think of it as having an honest and effortless give-receive relationship with Life.

PART II: Setting Yourself Up for Success

Chapter Ten: Frequently Asked Questions

How do I know this will work for me? Trust the process. The flow of your own honest expression, step-by-step, will reveal what you need to understand. Set the intention that you will clear your pattern with this practice. Know that you will. You will be naming as many thoughts and beliefs that pertain to your pattern as possible. The more aspects you can acknowledge about your pattern, the more it will help your mind to re-evaluate it enough to let it go. You will be moving a lot of energy with this practice. Knowing and intending that you are releasing trapped energy helps that energy to move out. Then you will fill in those spaces with brand new thoughts and beliefs that make your heart smile.

What is a pattern? A pattern is an experience, a behavior, a negative thought or habit that has happened repeatedly, and is causing you to struggle. This process may be applied to any pattern you have. What matters is you are able to identify it enough to name it. For example, you might name your pattern the *overeating* pattern, the *always late for work* pattern, the *rejection* pattern, the *low self-esteem* pattern, the *fear* pattern, *attracting a mean boss* pattern, *dating the wrong person* pattern, the *financial* pattern, or the *anger* pattern, to name a few. Naming your pattern something specific can be healing by itself.

Where do I start? Start with the most bothersome, painful, burning issue first. The issue bothering you the most is the highest priority issue to address. Painful usually means louder and when a pattern is loud, it is easier to clear. The louder the pattern, the more ready you are to release it. Plus, the louder the pattern, the more clearly you can hear and sense the way it talks to you.

Can I address all my issues at once? In this practice, we address one pattern at a time. To successfully clear out one whole pattern of related thinking you will need to stay on topic and keep the pattern bounded and referenced to the original pattern throughout the journaling process. Do your best to resist going on tangents. Tangents disperse the energy too much. It is the very nature of painful energy to distract its captive from the core issue so that you don't clear it. Your pattern wants to live; it wants to continue to have its life through you. We want to end its life. Staying on topic and writing just enough to capture the energy of each message will give you a clean release of a whole system of related energy.

How do I keep the focus on myself when it seems my pattern is about someone else? Perception is a funny thing. Circumstances that seem so real can be totally false. Often our perception is nothing more than our own projected assumptions about what we think happened, not what actually occurred. Projections show up everywhere in patterns. To guard against getting caught up in a projection, keep the focus entirely on yourself and your own experience. For example, it's fine to write down someone's judgment about you and how their judgment impacts you, but be clear in your heart it is your assumption about what he or she thinks about you. Owning your own experience throughout this entire process, blaming no one and making no assumptions, is the best way to clear out negative energy. The point of power is always within you.

Can I use my electronic devices for this? I highly recommend writing by hand during this process. I have found paper-and-pen is more personal and is energetically quieter than using electronic devices. True, it's easier to go back and fill in thoughts in previous Discovery Prompts when subsequent prompts spark new ideas, but it is not worth the ease of organization to give up the quiet, organic stillness of pen and paper. Since writing is slower, it offers space to feel what you write. Acknowledgment of feelings is often the solution itself and leads to identifying other valuable feelings and insights. We do this by writing one thought at a time, by hand, on paper. This is also a good way to stimulate the voice of the child you once were. Many of us first held a crayon in our hand to express ourselves.

What kind of paper should I use? Use whatever allows you to be the most honest with yourself. If a fancy, expensive journal causes you to feel you have to be more poetic or polite, or that you have to have perfect handwriting, then don't use one. You need to be able to write sloppily if you want to, to misspell words you don't know and to say things you typically feel you aren't allowed to say. You need a place to write sentences that don't make sense to anyone but you. I use a standard legal pad. I use it for every journal entry I make whether it's for recording my dreams or clearing patterns. I put everything, one entry after another, onto that one pad until it's full. I write the beginning date on the front page and when it's full I add the end date. Then I put it away in a special place and start a new one.

You may want to draw a logo on the front of your journal, some image evoking the core goodness you feel about yourself. This symbol is as valuable as seeing a logo or picture of your favorite singer or band. The logo on their album says something special, or should, about their music.

Your logo, if you choose to use one, should evoke your own heart's song in the most positive way, calling you to write with yourself.

Use the most comfortable pen you have, one that glides.

Note: You may download a free copy of The Lotus Flower Living Companion Journal (.pdf) at LotusFlowerLiving.com/Book, by validating the purchase of this book.

How do I organize my pattern messages? Although there are steps to this process and they are presented in an order designed to assist your mind to let the pattern go, it doesn't matter how you write them down. If you are on Discovery Prompt 5 and you get more insight into Discovery Prompt 2, you may go back to add that new insight if there is still room on the page. Or, you can simply write it down in Discovery Prompt 5. What matters is you acknowledge it by writing it down. What you write only needs to make sense to you. The messages you write down only need to register enough for you to feel them.

How much time should I allow? Once you've read the entire book, please allow a few hours for your first session of clearing work. This way you will be able to get through an entire pattern at once giving your mind, heart and body the chance to experience what a full pattern let-go can feel like. It feels exhilarating to go start-to-finish on an entire pattern in one sitting. By allowing enough time to finish, it will be easier to stay with your original pattern all the way through the Discovery Prompts. Plus, you will have positive expectations in *body memory* working in your favor the next time you sit down to address a pattern.

There may come a time when you can sit down to clear your pattern in thirty minutes or less knowing exactly which Discovery Prompts to use, but I would recommend going through all the Discovery Prompts for your first five to ten pattern-clearing sessions at least. I want to say the first twenty-five sessions – because sometimes a pattern message will tell you to skip an essential prompt just to trick you and it takes practice to learn this. Self-deception takes many forms. We all have blind spots. And patterns can be sneaky and slick.

What I do is just begin, even if I only intend to devote a half hour to the process, and next thing I know two hours have passed and I have cleared an entire pattern. However, don't let my time suggestions stop you from getting started. Just start.

What can I expect? Expect to be surprised by what you hear, feel and sense. Expect the messages to be every version and mixture of truth and lie you can imagine. They will be. That's normal. Expect some of the pattern's logic to sound ridiculous. Just laugh and be curious. Wonder what your pattern has to say. Listen to it and write it down. This is really all we are doing here. Detached curiosity with a bit of humor and lots of honesty works well.

The more honest, neutral and objective you can be as you face your pattern's messages, the more false messages you will be able to identify and to clear out. Some of the messages will be sad. There may be moments when you will need to cry. That's also normal. Let yourself have a moment of tears. That is pain energy being released. Allow it to release, take a moment to process, and keep going. Don't let it completely take you out of your neutral mind-set. Just let it move through you.

You may also notice that writing down certain thoughts causes you to take a spontaneous, deep breath. That's when you know you have hit a message with a lot of meaning and emotional charge. By all means, do pause during those moments to let the awareness sink in, and to allow the once trapped energy to move off. That's the point.

Will writing negative truth perpetuate more negative truth? Although this practice requires a willingness to identify your negative truth, you can know just by writing it down, you will not be creating more negative truth. Because your intention is to clear out negative truth, clearing out negative truth is what you will be doing. The overall intention here is to create a new way of being in the world, a new way of thinking, feeling and behaving. To do that, we will be giving voice to those messages in a *discovery and release* kind of way.

Is it okay for me to combine this process with other modalities I like to use? Yes, please do. For example, if you have a particular personality-typing framework you enjoy, such as the Enneagram or Myers-Briggs, and if those frameworks help you delve deeper into this work, that's brilliant. If you understand birth-order and how it impacts your perception, you may bring that knowledge to this process. If you are well versed in the power centers in the body, the chakras, and know which of your power centers tend to be out of balance, then fold that knowledge about yourself into this work. If you enjoy astrology and know your astrological makeup, then apply that information. If you enjoy flower essences or essential oils and want to use them while you engage in this process, I highly encourage it.

Chapter Eleven: Primary Objectives of This Practice

As we learned in Part I, the Lotus Flower Living Journaling Practice clears out limiting beliefs by making known the pattern of *thought-logic* central to a particular issue, giving your mind and heart a chance to make new decisions.

The goal of this writing practice is to give you clarity about a problem that is currently bothering you. Our highest intention is to give you a sense of completion and balance, bringing your mind to a place of stillness.

Throughout the 16 Discovery Prompts in the chapters that follow, there are three primary objectives:

1. Tap into the joy of your Highest Intention, imagining it as though it already exists.

2. Clear out everything that doesn't support or agree with the essence of your Highest Intention.

3. Claim your New Truth to anchor your new awareness.

You Will Be Contrasting Two Opposing Concepts at Once

Perhaps the most complex aspect of this work is that I will ask you to switch back and forth between two distinct mind-sets throughout the steps. The first: your Highest Intention – how you wish life to be after you clear your pattern. And, the second: your current issue – how it feels right now.

We begin with the end goal in mind. The end goal is how you imagine life will be for you without your issue. You will be comparing and contrasting the joy you imagine feeling, living free of your issue, against how your issue currently feels. In doing this, you actively engage your faith in your Highest Intention to shine a light on your issue.

We do this comparison between these two distinct feelings because it highlights the details of the pattern and keeps the entire clearing process contained and on topic.

Actively comparing and contrasting between your felt experiences of these two realities strengthens the one that is based in Spiritual Truth and negates the one that is based in illusion. It is also effective because it is exactly like saying a positive affirmation such as *I love myself*, hearing voices in your head arguing back why you are not lovable, and then writing down what you hear.

Tapping into one's faith in a highest potential outcome while saddled with the despair of a painful issue can feel impossible if you are not accustomed to working with affirmations. Yet, without at least a sense of what you want to receive before you begin, you will end up working in circles.

If you need to prepare your mind for this practice, you may find it helpful to light a candle, to make yourself a cup of tea, or to sit on your favorite meditation cushion for a moment, to find the place in you that knows, feels and believes there is life beyond this issue.

Do what you need to do to find a neutral space in your heart that is receptive to a new experience. A new experience does exist and it doesn't matter at all if you don't know exactly what it looks like. In fact, it's best to not be too rigid about how it might look, rather to be open to the idea that a delightful solution does exist, and that the flow of your own beautiful expression will reveal it to you. Being open to possibility alone is enough.

Chapter Twelve: Creating a Receptive Mind-Set

Care is being taken here to ensure your success with this clearing work. The goal is for you to have a powerful first pattern-clearing experience, and many more to follow. I offer the following mind-sets and points for your consideration.

Purity of intention: Before you start to clear a pattern, I would encourage you to be clear and specific on what you want to experience. Check, and recheck, the purity of your intention. A pure intention will never cause you to attempt to manipulate others or to get love from outside yourself. A pure intention never infringes on anyone else. A pure intention increases your love and respect for yourself and doesn't require anyone else to change in order for you to be happy. There is plenty for everyone, including you, and if you are meant to have a new way of being in the world, you will have it.

*Worthiness***:** To invest the kind of self-focused time required for this work, you will need to see yourself as worthy enough to invest this time. Therefore, you need a sense of self-worth before you begin. It takes self-esteem to build more self-esteem. If you do not have self-value, then you will not have a reference point for creating more self-value. A quick way to plant seeds of self-worth is to place your hands in the center of your chest and say the word *precious*. The word *precious* activates a sense of kindness and worth.

*Gratitude***:** For perspective it helps to anchor ourselves in what is good before we begin to clear a pattern. Something is always going well somewhere in one's life. When we take a moment to find goodness, we feel more secure and connected, and connection encourages flow. When we practice gratitude, it centers us in a sense that all is well and reminds us of our ability to create and receive. In essence, we are acknowledging life is reciprocal; that we are a vital part of this cycle and no matter what patterns we have, life is good.

You are not your patterns: The patterns you will be clearing are nothing more than patterns. They are not who you are. Who you are, as a spiritual being, is far greater than the patterns you will be clearing out. The reason certain issues appear unsolvable is because up until now you have likely been too identified with them. Think of your pattern in terms of size. In sessions with clients I often draw a large circle, point to it and say – *This is you.* Then I draw a tiny circle and say – *This is your pattern.* That is not to say your pattern doesn't cause you a lot of trouble. It is just that it helps to have perspective so you don't get overwhelmed. While it is true we are each responsible for our every belief, thought and action, we are not, in and of itself, any belief, thought or action. We are more powerful than our patterns, and spiritually speaking, we are already perfect just the way we are.

Non-judgment: The most intimate relationship you will ever have is the one you have with yourself. As with any intimate relationship, non-judgment is how we keep communication flowing. If a child came to you wanting to share something hurtful that happened at school, you wouldn't judge him for sharing how he handled the situation. You would encourage him to tell the full story. We want the voices of our patterns to *talk* to us. If we judge what we discover too harshly, we won't have the nerve to express it and to write it down. Acceptance of the issue is essential in order to fully let it go.

Privacy: Promise yourself before you begin journaling that no one will ever read what you write during your pattern-clearing session. It absolutely has to be private; otherwise your inner child won't feel safe enough to say what he or she needs to say. Commit to yourself before you begin, and often during your session, that this writing is just for you. Even if you have to tear up and discard your writing afterwards to be sure. No matter what it is, you get to say it here in a private space, writing with and to yourself. Nothing you say will be wrong. Here it is all okay. A sense of privacy allows for full honest expression, and full honest expression leads to freedom. Keeping your writing private does the trick.

Three practices for creating a safe, receptive attitude and space: Part of the reason you may not have been able to clear your pattern before now is because your pattern messages were likely too painful to hear. Pain causes us to resist what we hear. Therefore, we need to create a calm, neutral and stable space within ourselves to receive those messages. Here are three practices you can do to create this space.

Be grounded: Revisiting certain experiences and feelings may be upsetting and you may find yourself getting fuzzy or distracted, yet what is actually happening is you have become ungrounded. When working with patterns as a whole, as we will be doing, you will come across aspects that you feel, but don't remember. Since feelings are felt in the body, it is important to ground yourself before you attempt to clear a pattern. Being stable in your body will allow you to access the answers you will need to clear your pattern. You can do this by breathing deeply, and by taking a few moments to imagine roots growing out of your feet, extending deep into the earth. Once you sense these imaginary, energetic roots securely in the ground, breathe 'up' the energy of stability and let yourself feel well-rooted.

Bubble of light: Imagine you are completely surrounded by a large bubble of light that spans the fingertips of your outstretched arms, or larger. Imagine the outer membrane of this bubble is a smart-filter about 2 – 3 inches thick that automatically filters out everything except the vibration of pure love. Inside this bubble you are completely safe. All thoughts are your own. Imagine your bubble is filled with qualities you'll need to assist you with your pattern, things like intuition, balance, safety, wisdom, humor, neutrality, positive self-regard, love, and peace.

Call in higher support: In order to access the answers needed to do this work, it is important to feel safe. Pattern-clearing sessions can be taken over by distortion and distraction so it is helpful to call in your higher spiritual resources before you begin.

If you are asking – *Who or what is my higher spiritual support?* In short, this support is evident everywhere. We've all had those wondrous moments that let us know we're not alone – witnessing a spectacular sunrise or sunset that brings tears to your eyes, a poignant dream that stays with you for days, a wise voice heard just as you are waking up, or some synchronistic event saving you from a sudden mishap that leaves you with a definite feeling you are being looked after. People call this presence many things: God, Goddess, the Source of All Life, or Divine Love Itself. You may also call on your angels and guides, invoke your own Higher Self as a guiding light, or your own beloved Soul as a higher source of support and protection. Many people also like to call in their ancestors for certain patterns.

It doesn't matter what you call the positive presences that help to guide your life. What matters is that you acknowledge you do have higher guidance available to you, and that you take a moment to invite this guidance to join you during your session. We never know what we will discover as we work on our patterns, just as at night we never know what dreams we might have. We won't know until we start to explore. So, I recommend starting this work with a sense of protection and safety by inviting in a presence that feels insightful, comforting and protective. You might say something like this –

> *I invite my higher spiritual support to guide my clearing work today and to help me stay on track. Please hold me in a space of safety, balance and protection at all times. Help me to be courageous and open, and please help me sense the answers clearly. Thank you.*

Look how much you have learned. Probably several different kinds of patterns have been speaking up while you read Parts I and II. We only address one pattern at a time. Which one will it be? Many blessings to you as you turn the page to clear your first pattern.

PART III: The Lotus Flower Living Journaling Practice

Chapter Thirteen: Discovery Prompt 1
State the Issue

You know you have a pattern when you feel a familiar kind of toxic pain. It burns. It's gut wrenching. You may hear yourself say, *this always happens to me, people always treat me this way,* or *I can't believe I did that again,* or *I can't believe I said that again.* You may feel dumbfounded, not sure what just happened. You may want to blame someone else for how you feel. You may feel defensive. You may find yourself in a circular state of justification about why you did what you did, going back and forth evaluating both sides of an issue, not able to resolve it. You may be adamant about your opinion, yet sticking with it doesn't feel good at all. Strong reactions are often clues to patterns.

The way to lotus flower peace is to tell yourself the truth. No one ever has to read this. This is just you having a moment of truth with yourself. Freedom can begin now with this Discovery Prompt by getting the issue down on paper. What are you wrestling with? What confuses you? What hurts? What is going on?

No issue is too small or too big to bring to the table. I have brought every, and any, reaction I ever wanted to soothe: every health problem – and I had many; every relationship confusion; every time I tried to get love from outside myself (instead of generating my own self-love) or engaged in any codependent behavior; or any time I felt unloved or unsafe, I brought it to this process and let the Discovery Prompts reveal a deeper understanding about my thinking. If it bothered me, I named it, and brought it here.

What is on your mind? What gives you an unsettled feeling in your stomach? You can bring it here.

Which pattern to choose? You will want to address the loudest and most painful issue first. Reason being, patterns have a highest priority ranking and when you go after the loudest one first, it is both easier to clear, and helps to dislodge the patterns beneath it. If you choose to work on a less painful situation just to get your feet wet, it won't be as effective, and you won't feel the powerful release as much.

I want you to experience the joy of your pattern going whoosh, right out the door, because then you will have those positive body memories working in your favor the next time you sit down to clear a pattern. So, what issue troubles you more than any other right now? That's the place to start.

You may find, as you proceed through the Discovery Prompts, the issue shifts in your understanding from the way you initially wrote it down.

That's fine. In fact, that is good. It means you are getting a clearer grasp of the issue. You can go back and write down your new awareness in this Discovery Prompt if there is still room or you may note it in the Discovery Prompt you are currently addressing. Put an asterisk by it or circle it noting – *This is the real issue.* If you are writing and feeling at the same time, you are doing it correctly. Just write your truth at the moment and keep breathing.

Help is on its way. Feeling better, clearer, safer and more secure is close at hand. Call in your spiritual support, feel their unconditional love for you – it is there – and let's begin.

Your Journaling Prompt:

Let your own loving spirit drop into your body as you answer the question – *What am I currently experiencing?* Name the problem. Feel the issue in your body and let it tell you what bothers you about it. Qualify the energy you are experiencing by naming how you feel. Describe the scene.

What is happening when you are doing what you wish you weren't doing?

Who is there? What is your reaction? What are the thoughts you wish you were not thinking? What is the behavior you wish you could change?

You can't do this wrong. The only wrong move is to avoid writing it down. You are always far wiser and more powerful than any pattern you will ever face. Even though your pattern may be painful, it is still smaller and less powerful than the full scope and power of you. Describe the issue just as you sense it. Write down at least five sentences, or more if you can, and remember to breathe.

This writing is only for you. This is your sacred alone time, wrapped in the unconditional love of your higher guidance. Whatever you write is perfectly fine. Getting it down will stop the energy from swirling. You are safe. Write five sentences or more if you can. This is how you change your life.

Welcome back. Getting started is the hardest part. Good for you for putting words to your issue and getting it down on paper. Good for you for daring to live life in a new way and for trusting that you can change your life. Clearing patterns is possible and you are now on your way. Great job!

Please turn the page where we will spend a few moments imagining how great life is going to be without your pattern. Hint: It's going to be amazing!

Chapter Fourteen: Discovery Prompt 2
Set Your Highest Intention

We begin with the end in mind – you cannot create something out of nothing. It takes a spark to create fire. It takes seed, soil and water to grow a plant. In this process, it takes a little faith and imagination.

You have stated the issue and now you are going to identify how you want to feel once your issue is resolved. Use your imagination to tap into the highest possible outcome for your issue. What would life feel like without this issue? How wondrous would life be if you could wake up tomorrow and feel extraordinarily different in a tangible way? How would you think? How would you behave? What would be different? How would you treat yourself differently? How would you treat others differently? How would life be better for you? What new sense of freedom would you have? How would your body change? What new skill or strength would you have?

Draw from whatever you can to get a sense of a greater possibility. If you can picture in your mind or can find a picture in a magazine of someone whose presence represents what you want to experience, use that. If you can center your mind on an absolute essence such as peace, joy or abundance or any other spiritual concept, do that. The energy you draw to yourself in this Discovery Prompt is the energy that will move into your deeper awareness after the pattern is cleared. This energy, and more like it, will fill the void after the old thought pattern has been cleared out.

An effective intention is one that feels joyful, exciting and freeing to you. Ask yourself – *In light of my core issue, what do I want to experience instead?* When you have the central question, you can find your highest intention.

Often though, we don't nail the true essence of what we actually want. For example, you may think you want a promotion at work and so you choose *getting a promotion at work* as your highest intention. Again, the point of power is always within us. Usually, when an intention presents to us as something coming to us from outside ourselves such as acknowledgment granted from another person, it is something deeper that we want. Setting an intention such as getting a promotion at work is limited.

Therefore, to find the more open-ended intention, the next question you would ask is – *How would having a promotion cause me to feel?* The answer might be a feeling of security, a sense of value, a sense of belonging, or increased self-respect. Unlike the intention of getting a promotion at work, these are powerhouse intentions. The Universe works well with pure, open intentions like these.

To distill an intention down to its purest form, you might ask – *If this intention comes true, what will it give to me and how will I feel when I receive it?* If the answer is, increased self-respect, then you would work your pattern around this intention, which would open the field of where your pattern-clearing session can go. You might keep it contained to work-related subjects, or you might just center on how lack of self-respect has played out as a pattern in your life in general.

Another reason we begin with the end in mind is because receiving new awareness is a skill at the level of accepting, and not blocking, new energy coming to us. The old energy you will be clearing out may be painful, but it *is* familiar. The energy you will be bringing in to take its place will have a higher vibration and may feel foreign to you, and so it helps to get acquainted with it before you begin.

A common example to explain why we might block a higher frequency of energy, even though it is a better energy, is the example of the person who had previously been in a dysfunctional relationship who begins dating a new healthy, functional person. Because the previous relationship was the original benchmark, he or she may have a difficult time accepting and being attracted to a healthy person. It can feel weird. It's a new experience. This is how it can be with new patterns. We have to invite the energy in and do our part to become comfortable with it.

Your body doesn't know the difference between what's real or imagined; therefore, breathing into your intention and feeling it with your emotional body gives your words power. Once you nail down the feeling of what you want to experience, feeling it as though it already exists, you say – *Okay, Divine Spirit of Pure Potentiality, who has no judgment about what I ask for, I claim this or something better.* There it is: the feeling is anchored and a contract with The Divine is made.

There's a moment during an effective, co-creative experience when we release our intention with complete knowing and trust. It's an innocent, relaxed, pure-hearted, time-stands-still, joyous moment where we send out our purest vibe, sensing what we know we can and will have. We feel grateful as though we have already received it. We completely detach. This is where the energy gets moving. The more fully we release our attachment to outcome, the better will be our manifestation. We don't necessarily know what will happen, but we trust it will be good because our intention is pure. Having pure intentions, and knowing when our intentions aren't pure, is what matters. There is no blame, fault or judgment. As we learned earlier, there is only cause and effect. There is only *I love you, and yes.*

In this Discovery Prompt, you acknowledge spiritually you are whole and perfect. You are sitting securely on the Lotus Flower, peaceful, stable and at ease, full of joy and vitality. There is nothing wrong with you. You are always okay no matter what is going on. We need this stability as we look at patterns because it gives us perspective, it reminds us of True Reality, and it provides a counterbalance to the sheer negativity of our patterns.

Please take a moment to call in your spiritual support, remind yourself that this writing is just for you, and let yourself imagine a joyous outcome. No dream or vision or wish is silly. If you want it and can picture it, and it brings goodness to all involved without harming anyone, you can have it.

Your Journaling Prompt:

State your Highest Intention in the form of a powerful, present tense statement. Write down at least five sentences claiming your intention for your clearing work. My life without this pattern will look and feel like _____.

For example, if your intention is to create more self-love and self-approval, you would write –

I now love and approve of myself just the way I am. I now release all that is in the way of loving and approving of myself. My experiences from now on reflect to me the love and approval I have for myself. I easily embrace the love that comes to me as a reflection of the love I have for myself. It feels wonderful to embrace a deeper inner love.

As you are writing your Highest Intention, feel this truth in your body, and take one long, deep breath. You're telling the power within you and around you –

This is what I am intending. I can have this. I believe it. I claim this or something better or whatever is for the highest good. I am open to receive.

Now that you have named the issue and have stated your highest intention, you have two powerful reference points. From here you will contrast your feelings back and forth to evoke the limited beliefs that typically work against manifesting your highest good. We reference the negative truth against your Highest Intention for perspective. We will revisit both of these Discovery Prompts throughout the entire practice to keep the work specific to your goal and to make sure the aspects we cover hit your targeted concern.

Great job! You are learning to work with emotional energy in a practical, functional way. Using contrast to distinguish what you want from what you do not want is like choosing the emotional radio dial you most want to be tuned into. By doing the Discovery Prompts that follow, you will be clearing out emotional energy and anchoring new energy which will allow the experience you most want to have – all because you are doing the real work now.

You are now ready to dive into Discovery Prompt 3, where we flip the switch and start the clearing work.

Chapter Fifteen: Discovery Prompt 3
Identify Your Pattern's Limiting Beliefs

You are doing great. You are still here. I am here, too, cheering you on, getting ready to ask you questions to stimulate your thought process in regard to your pattern. This is where I want to encourage you to drop into your body yet another level and be very present with yourself. In this Discovery Prompt, it is time to do a huge purge to write as many thoughts and feelings as we can, allowing our pattern to talk to us. Our pattern messages bother us for good reasons. They want to be heard. They want to have their time to speak. That time is now.

With the excitement of how life can be without your issue fresh on the page (Discovery Prompt 2), you have something to compare and to push against. You now have a new standard of how life can be written out before you and can let this new vision illuminate the limiting messages and behaviors of your pattern. The messages of your pattern, which may, at times, consist of false or exaggerated facts, will be more obvious in comparison to your Highest Intention. The mind says – *Wait a minute, this is what I can have and this is what I actually do have. Okay, let's address this.*

Just a reminder from Chapter Two – pattern messages are fueled by the collective unconscious pain-body, as well as by our own pain energy, that is, our own past pain history. They are not the full truth, yet we need to honor them and nail them down and hear what they typically say to us.

You are not alone here. You have your spiritual guidance with you. You have your commitment to your Highest Intention and you have your trustworthy cellular body memory, which we will rely on heavily in this prompt. And, you have me. I have been here many times doing this same process and I will be here guiding you every step of the way.

Here we let the voices of our pattern land on paper. As you think about your pattern, feel your feelings in your body. Like we learned in the section on Body Memory, it helps to identify your feelings first and then work backward to grasp the thought that fuels the feeling. Where do you feel the feeling in your body? Do you feel it in your heart, head or gut? Thoughts happen lightning fast, so trust your instincts and listen deeply to yourself.

I offer you three examples to get your writing juices going. Example one is Karen, who is obsessing about missing her ex-husband and her intention is to be free of these obsessive thoughts. Example two is Victoria, who is struggling to lose weight, and who just came back to her senses after a three-day eating binge. Her intention is to discover what triggers her eating surges so she can take weight off and keep it off. Example three is Howard, who wants to stop overreacting to his family members at the holidays. His intention is to come back from family visits feeling happy with his own behavior.

The stream-of-consciousness thoughts and beliefs you generate in this Discovery Prompt will be reference points to guide you, when you need inspiration, as you proceed through the prompts. You can always come back to your writings in this prompt when you get stuck. So, write like the wind, and remember just because you listed a pattern message doesn't mean it is actually true. It may be completely irrational and that's expected. This is how you make that determination. Let it come out of you and onto the page.

Be careful about going on tangents. Give each thought a moment, feel it and breathe. Think of it as an interview process. You are the interviewer and the pattern is the guest on your show. Listen to what it has to say without any judgment and write exactly what you hear. I find it liberating to write what I hear in my patterns. I hope you do, too. This is your opportunity to say things you normally don't allow yourself to say or admit. Here it is okay. This is the place for expressing negative truth.

Karen's intention is peace of mind about her ex-husband. She wants freedom from her obsessive thoughts. In her stream of consciousness purge for Discovery Prompt 3, she writes:

> I feel like a fool. Am I in high school? I'm embarrassed. I feel like I am a weak person. I'm mad at myself for obsessing about this man.

I want my dignity back. (This is actually a great intention sentence so we could move it to step two or circle it.)

My pattern tells me I'm a phony. I'm having a lot of memories about his kids and I'm afraid of what their father has told them about me.

I want them to know I am a good person. My pattern tells me I am a bad person.

I feel sad about losing all these associated relationships.

I tell myself I am not lovable. No one wants me.

I obsess about wanting an apology from him.

I fantasize about him apologizing to me, sincerely from his heart. We hug, we kiss and we get back together. He has never done this. Why would I expect that?

Victoria's intention is to stop binge eating so she can maintain a healthy weight. In her journaling pages, she writes:

It happened again. I was doing so well. I had lost 20 pounds.

When my boss criticized me at work, I came home feeling lost and depressed.

I heard myself say, I can't do anything right.

I feel deep grief in my gut right now.

At the time though I didn't feel it, I stuffed it. I didn't want to feel my feelings. I wanted to forget. I wanted to eat. I felt numb.

Dieting takes too much concentration. It takes too much energy.

I hear my pattern say I'm not lovable. I'm not worthy. I'm not capable. I will never reach my goal. I will never be thin. I will never have love in my life. I will always be alone and I will always be fat. I don't have the determination. I hear I can't do this. I can't have what I want.

I'm disappointed with myself.

Howard's intention is to stop overreacting to his family members' behavior when he visits. He writes:

I got tripped up again. My pattern tells me I am being set up.

I hear that I am being scapegoated.

What happens is, in a moment of wanting a connection, I try too hard.

I get scared. My need for my family's love and approval causes me to say the wrong thing. I sabotage myself.

I go there expecting different results, but the same thing always happens. I want love and I feel rejected. My pattern tells me I am unworthy. I hear it say that this time it will be different, so go ahead try it again and then again, I sabotage myself. I overreacted when my brother inquired about my work.

I feel betrayed by both my family and myself.

These are short examples and they are somewhat mild. When I do this step, I will compile a full page or two of pattern messages. Remember if your pattern speaks to you in a very nasty voice and uses foul language write it down that same way. We want to acknowledge the way you hear, feel, sense and experience it.

Do your best to stay on topic. Refer to your issue in Discovery Prompt One whenever you need some direction. If you find yourself blaming someone else for how you feel, for example, if you write – *My brother intended to get me to react by bringing up my job* – try starting your sentence with one of these phrases:

My perception is…

I tell myself…

My assumption is…

Phrases like these allow you to state your messages with ownership, instead of blame. The more you can identify, the more you can clear out.

Take a moment now to breathe in the beauty of your own perfection. All you want to be exists in the All Possible. The spirit that is you is whole, peaceful and stable always. Here we are merely dealing with pattern messages. They are not you. You are far more than any message you will write down. Call in higher guidance, surround yourself with a sense of safety, breathe in your strength and let's get going.

Your Journaling Prompt:

Please list 15 to 25 or more lies, messages, limiting beliefs, truths, half-truths, full truths, distorted facts, real facts – anything and everything negative about your pattern. Just jot down sentences and thoughts here, staying on topic. Use "I" statements that allow you to own your experience. For example – *It tells me I am _____ (stupid, ineffective, worthless, etc.). I feel _____ about this issue.*

Feel your feelings fully and write as fast as you can to allow the negative voices of your pattern to speak. Consider how far back some of these messages go. Hold your inner child securely in your heart. No one ever has to read this. This is only for you. Get it out and onto the page. You can do this. Tell your truth.

Welcome back. You are powerful. Your words, thoughts and behaviors are important. As you evolve and change your patterns, you assist many others by your example alone. This is brave, generous, and healing work you are doing for yourself and for all who love you. Thank you for doing this work. I hope you are feeling a sense of relief. Expressing the negative truth of your pattern will set you free. Stay with me as we untangle this issue further in Discovery Prompt 4.

Chapter Sixteen: Discovery Prompt 4
Seek Out Your Pattern's Hiding Strategies

As you think about the issue you identified in Discovery Prompt 1, take heart, as there are reasons why your pattern may have been difficult to identify before now. Patterns use hiding strategies in the form of thoughts and behaviors you might not associate with your pattern, such as avoidance and compensating behaviors that distract you from the real issue.

Think of hiding strategies as the tip of your pattern's iceberg. While these behaviors are patterns of their own, their purpose is to either distract you from, help you cope with, or cause you to avoid a more complicated issue. For example, procrastination can be a hiding strategy for a fear pattern; or, consider the friend who complains about the same problem over and over with no interest in solving the real issue. Complaining is a hiding strategy her pattern is using to avoid and to cope with her issue.

As we go through the prompts we will be chipping away at the large iceberg below the surface. What helps us to do that is to identify specific thoughts and actions that, up until now, have distracted us from the true issue.

Included in this definition are exaggerated personality traits, whereby these traits get all the fanfare; meanwhile, the bigger pattern never gets addressed. To fully untangle and clear your pattern, we take care to acknowledge the hiding strategies it uses because it helps our mind take notice there is more going on here than meets the eye.

Hiding strategies can be behaviors that cause you to defend your issue. For example, if you are addressing a people-pleasing codependency pattern, perhaps your pattern asserts – *I am not codependent, I am just a nice person.* Therefore, the thought – *I'm just a nice person* – is a hiding strategy for the codependency issue.

If you are addressing an overeating pattern and you often hear the message – *I need to keep eating to make sure I get enough nutrition* – your pattern may be using this message to continue eating when honestly, you've already had enough food for the day.

Denial is a classic hiding strategy. If you are working on an addiction pattern and you hear the message – *It is not that I can't quit this habit, rather my pattern tells me I don't have a problem.* In this case, the hiding strategy is the message – *I don't think I have a problem* – or you can just write *denial of the real issue.*

Hiding strategies can also be any thought or behavior that help you to compensate for the larger pattern. Let's say you are addressing a pattern which involves feeling insecure in relationships. A hiding strategy might be that you compensate by withholding information from the other person or you might compensate by continually obsessing about the other person's behavior, looking for reasons to justify feeling insecure.

A hiding strategy might be the way your pattern causes you to *use other people*, such as complaining or playing the victim. It might cause you to use other people by lying or cause you to have an uncontrollable urge to be the center of attention or cause you to make your own emotional care someone else's responsibility. Think of the person who chronically puts herself down, so others will say – *No, you are wonderful, really.*

Hiding strategies can also be thoughts and behaviors that are perfectly fine and healthy yet your pattern is exaggerating them. *Personality traits* fall into this category. For example, the tendency to be shy, or to take charge of things, or to be cautious, or to be sensitive are all fine traits when in balance. They only become hiding strategies when they are out of balance.

Does your tendency to be extroverted or introverted come into play with your pattern? Maybe you are achievement-oriented, but this trait, as it relates to your pattern, causes you to neglect your family. Maybe your personality is upbeat and positive, but it causes you to avoid addressing negative topics.

Your hiding strategies might look like a list of words. Perhaps you have a leaning toward *self-doubt*, *procrastination*, or *fear of making a mistake*. Maybe you *worry*. If so, you might write – *self-doubt*, *procrastination*, *fear* and *worry*.

Emotions can be hiding strategies as well: shame, resentment, anger, fear, anxiety, and panic, etc. Low self-esteem, in fact, is a common hiding strategy. Even positive emotions can be hiding strategies depending on how your pattern is using them.

What is great about identifying hiding strategies, in the scope of the whole pattern, is that any hiding strategy you name will be balanced out at the end of the journaling prompts when you clear your pattern. To me it feels like getting a personality upgrade without having to work each individual trait on its own. Keep in mind nothing real is ever lost in clearing work. True gifts remain and all else is harmonized.

As you think about your pattern, here are some questions to consider:

> How does your pattern cause you to avoid certain tasks, events, people or activities?

> How do you avoid dealing with the real issue?

> How do you compensate for your pattern? What thoughts or behaviors do you engage in to compensate for the way your pattern causes you to feel?

> What kinds of excuses does your pattern offer, which in turn, distracts you from addressing it?

> What are your pattern's coping mechanisms? What do you do to make yourself feel better?

> Does your pattern cause you to use other people in your coping strategies? If so, what do you do?

How does your pattern cause you to defend your behaviors, thoughts and attitudes? You might find yourself naming addictions as hiding strategies since addictions are often a way that we cope with deeper issues. No worries if your answers repeat on other Discovery Prompts. It is good to have overlap.

Whether or not this is the first time you have asked yourself these questions in regard to your pattern, you know these answers. The moment you ask the questions, the answers appear. Trust what you hear, feel or sense. Anything you write down is fine, even if it is a guess.

Remember you are not alone. Take a moment to connect with your higher spiritual support. There is comfort and help immediately nearby. There is no judgment about hiding strategies. There is only neutral self-observation and a sense of curiosity. Staying in your adult, objective mind-set, you may wish to bring your inner child along, holding his or her hand, as you think about how far back some of these hiding strategies go.

You are not your pattern, and you are not your personality and you are certainly not your hiding strategies. You are a bright spirit who is willing to evolve. Every person on the planet has patterns with hiding strategies, yet not everyone is willing to sit with paper and pen and ask their hiding strategies to reveal themselves. Take a deep breath, trust that you understand the task at hand, and with gentle, loving detachment listen, feel and observe what your pattern has to say.

Your Journaling Prompt:

List as many hiding strategies as you can think of, as they relate to your pattern. At a minimum try to name 15 ways your pattern causes you to avoid, compensate, cope or distract you from the real issue. Feel free to list more as you think of them. You already know the real issue because you named it in the first Discovery Prompt, so now it is just a matter of acknowledging the ways your pattern has, up until now, caused you to avoid and compensate for it.

With each hiding strategy you list, you are bringing awareness to your pattern. Awareness changes everything.

Welcome back. By naming your pattern's hiding strategies you are diffusing its power and control over you. It is no fun to play hide and seek if there is no place to hide. Now you are the one with the power, which you have had all along except now it will feel more tangible. Now you know how to spot hiding strategies. There is no need to work hard at this because here you are working smart. You are outsmarting your pattern with every Discovery Prompt you do. Excellent work!

Chapter Seventeen: Discovery Prompt 5
Voice Your Family Messages

At the level of your pattern, the family messages you received in childhood influence the ways you think about yourself and your life. In this Discovery Prompt you will identify limiting beliefs from your earliest familial roots that specifically feed your current issue. Of course, there will be good, healthy and productive family messages, too. Yet, here we are concerned about the negative and unproductive messages that influence and confuse the issue you are addressing.

Family loyalty runs deep. If you have never before considered how unhealthy beliefs and messages from your family of origin influence your belief system, this prompt may feel a bit foreign or harsh to you, as if you are being disloyal or disrespectful to your family. If you already know how your family has influenced your beliefs and have loving boundaries and healthy objectivity, then this prompt can help you to explore it further as it relates to the issue at hand.

It is important to point out in this prompt we are not blaming your family. Just like you, your family members have done the best they could with the information they had. I believe we choose our parents based on what we want to learn, and the beliefs that were passed down are perfect for the themes we wanted to explore and to overcome in this lifetime.

With all due respect, there comes a time when certain patterns of belief have run their course through our family and we don't want them to continue through us any longer. When this prompt is approached with a strong sense of personal responsibility, loving detachment and respect, you can't go wrong.

From a spiritual perspective you are always connected to your family members. Above all appearances there is only love. You will not be betraying your loved ones by calling out false beliefs that influence your pattern. All you are doing is cleaning out a closet and taking a look at what's inside. Just pull some beliefs out of the closet and see what you have. You are not dragging out old dusty garments to throw them at your family. This information is only for you so you can clear your pattern. You are merely taking inventory. Does the family message that says it is arrogant or selfish to love yourself still fit you? No? Okay. Simply write it down.

One way to think about family messages is to explore the ways you behaved in your family of origin in order to belong, to feel safe, or to get approval. For example, what messages did you receive about your value, your intelligence, and your likability? How did you learn to communicate, to observe others and yourself?

The messages we received about ourselves in childhood can run the gamut. Most importantly, as you look at your pattern, what messages did you receive specifically that may have confused or distorted or reinforced your current issue?

Be careful to avoid getting pulled into the pain of any hurtful family messages. This is an adult process that requires you to be lovingly detached and observant. So please tread carefully here.

I would be remiss not to mention that any group to which you have ever belonged can act as a family environment, influencing the way you evaluate yourself, and that energy can stick. Therefore, you might consider high school, college, work, religious, or social groups. When you are working on a particularly troubling issue, you would be doing a thorough job to reference every group to which you have ever belonged where similar behavioral patterns were present.

Now might be a good time to refer back to your Highest Intention in Discovery Prompt 2 for how you'd like your life to be after your issue is resolved. Refresh your mind with the joy, peace and freedom you have claimed for yourself. Use this reference point for contrast to identify family messages that do not support your desired experience. Do keep it specific to your issue so you can stay on track.

This writing is just for you. No one ever has to read it. It is a worksheet where you can make discoveries and clear out energy. Let your pen lead the way as you listen for the family messages in your pattern. Call in your higher guidance. Breathe, breathe, breathe in a sense of safety and let's begin.

Your Journaling Prompt:

Recall the family messages that influence your issue. As you think of them now, what messages no longer make sense? This is your life and you get to decide what you want to believe. Ask yourself – *In regard to my issue, my family tells me* _____.

As you think of your pattern, recall the ways you behaved in childhood to feel safe, to belong or to get approval. What messages did you embody about your value, your abilities, your intellect, your likability and your place in the world?

Depending on your type of pattern, it may be helpful to consider your placement in the family hierarchy? Who held the power? What messages did you adopt about where you stood in terms of power? What did you decide about yourself? What rights do you feel you have to change your life? Do you feel empowered to live the life you want to live?

If none of these examples fit your issue, ask the questions that do prompt deeper exploration for you about your family messages.

What other *family* type groups can you name that perpetuated similar negative beliefs? Name the group to which you belonged, and the opinion about yourself you took from it. Can you find a thread of similar beliefs that have followed you from group to group? If so, this is great. You will be giving yourself a lot of freedom by naming them.

Do your best to identify at least 10 to 15 family messages that influence your issue, yet do not stop at 15 if you get on a roll. The more you can name, the more you can transform.

As with each step of this process, your body is a trustworthy resource. It helps to feel the messages in your body. You will know you have identified a charged belief when you can't help but take a spontaneous, deep breath. Expect to be surprised by what you discover, and please do write them down.

🪷 🪷 🪷

Welcome back. You are strong and brave to face the family messages that influence your pattern. Not only are you freeing yourself from limiting beliefs, you are greatly helping your family. As you venture to evolve, it helps everyone to evolve. We all move forward together. Look at you leading the way. Great job!

Chapter Eighteen: Discovery Prompt 6
Consider Your Cultural Messages

Now that we have looked at your pattern's family messages, let's consider the cultural messages that influence the issue you wish to change. If our family of origin is a pond of beliefs we swim in, then our culture is the lake we swim in, and the world is our ocean. Cultural messages inform our patterns in obvious and not so obvious ways.

Cultural thinking can often be made up of shared, limited, biased and prejudiced opinions that patterns use to trick us into believing the way we believe is normal and right. We may subconsciously assume – *This way of thinking isn't dysfunctional; it's normal for my culture.* Meanwhile, going along with irrational cultural norms has consequences for our mind, body and spirit. If certain beliefs aren't sustainable over time, they will throw us off balance regardless of how popular they are. It can be difficult to pinpoint what is throwing us off exactly when it is a popularly held belief.

For example, if you are choosing to quit an unhealthy habit, you will identify all the cultural messages that promote it. You will identify any messages that give the impression your habit somehow makes you more appealing, or that it connects you to the right people, etc. The truth is, you can be connected to the right people without your habit. Here we are separating fact from fiction.

In the case of working on a codependency pattern, you might consider any cultural message that says you have no value as a person unless you are in a relationship. A common verse is – *You are nobody until somebody loves you.*

Many songs and movies perpetuate this message. The truth is you are valuable and worthy with or without a partner.

You might also consider the cultural message that says – *To feel loved you have to get someone else to love you.* The truth is we must all learn to love ourselves before we can ever truly receive satisfying love from someone else and have it register.

If you are someone who grew up in a different country than the one you currently live in, your pattern might be influenced by both cultures, not to mention the contrast between the two cultures and the issues these differences can cause.

So, what happens when your heart tells you a certain path is right for you, but your culture sends a different message? It can be difficult to find your own truth about your right and perfect path because the urge to belong is so strong. A sense of belonging is tied to the need to be loved, which is tied to survival. It sparks in us the quandary – how much am I willing to be seen as different from my culture and will my differences be acceptable? Can I forge my own path and still enjoy a sense of safety and belonging?

It took my husband and me ten years to decide whether or not to have kids. We did not identify with either side of the spectrum: those who were earnest in their desire to have children or those who were certain they did not want children. We didn't want to leave such an important life decision to chance. We wanted to make a conscious choice, and of course make the right choice for us. When we finally arrived at our decision not to have children, I realized I had subconsciously known all along this choice was the right path for me, yet because having children is such a strong cultural norm, my inner knowing had a tough time competing with it.

As you think of your pattern, take heart, as there may be deeply held beliefs from your culture so intertwined in its messaging, you may have to engage your keenest objectivity and observation skills to see it. Yet once you write down one cultural message it won't be long until you can identify others. And then you will be noticing them all the time, as you go about your life, saying – *Oh, that's a cultural message. I can make a choice about that. I can challenge that. I have free will.*

Take a moment to refer to your Highest Intention in Discovery Prompt 2. Reinvigorate your vision for your new life without your pattern. Refresh your mind with the joy, safety and ease you have claimed for yourself. Let this reference provide contrast to identify cultural messages that do not support your desired experience.

Remember to keep your writing on topic. We are going for a thorough, deep clearing here. Write the messages just as you hear them.

Now is the time to call in your higher spiritual support to guide the way, and to remind yourself this writing is for your eyes only. This is your sacred time to discover what is true for you. Take a breath and feel your feet solidly on the floor as you fine-tune your awareness to the cultural messages in your pattern. Trust you do know the answers, and let's begin.

Your Journaling Prompt:

Give yourself the freedom to express the cultural messages that cause you to think you can't have what you want, or that say you should want something that isn't right for you.

As you think about your pattern, in terms of your sense of belonging, what messages perpetuate your pattern's theme? What thoughts do you hear that distort and confuse your true, grounded, practical and spiritual sense of what is right for you?

Ask yourself – *In regard to my issue, my culture tells me_____.*

When you think of the thoughts and behaviors of your pattern, how does popular cultural thinking reinforce those thoughts and behaviors? What do you hear that tells you it is perfectly okay everyone thinks this way? Your own beautiful spirit always knows better. What do you hear versus what do you know?

Do your best to name at least 10 to 15 cultural messages that influence your issue and more if you can identify them.

Keep breathing, check in with your body wisdom often and please do write them down.

Welcome back. This is how you reinvent your life. You are doing it. You have just separated popular cultural messages from messages that are right for you. You are coming more into your authentic self with each false message you renounce. With each line you write you are stepping more solidly into your authentic life. Now you are no longer swimming in cultural messages that perpetuate your pattern. Others can think the way they want to think and you can think the way that is right for you and we can all live peacefully together. Congratulations. You are on your way. Well done.

Chapter Nineteen: Discovery Prompt 7
Acknowledge How Your Pattern Affects Your Body

Your body has been with you from day one. Your body has been a participant in everything you have ever thought, felt, said or done. It is the home and vehicle of your beautiful spirit. Without your body, simply put, you could not be here. Likewise, your body exists for you and if it weren't for your being, it would not be here either. Together you make living a human life possible.

Given that your body has been present for everything you have ever thought, felt, said or done, it is your friend, witness and counselor as you bravely delve into your emotional patterning. It has been here through it all. If you feel it, your body feels it. If you think it, your body feels the results of that thought. Given this, in clearing work, the body is your ally.

Just like with any close friend, one's words and actions impact the well-being of that friend. If a friend says loving, helpful things, you feel uplifted. If a friend says negative words to you, you feel sad and may even have to work harder to compensate for the impact of those words. If your friend has behaviors that impact you physically, then you have to use even more strategies to protect yourself and to find balance.

The body has its own quiet, subtle, unique wisdom. In pattern-clearing work, we acknowledge your body is a part of your journey. It has an opinion about how it is treated and is happy to share. In this Discovery Prompt, we ask the body how it has been affected and we listen with great interest.

There is no judgment here about what has come before. It is all just information. Here there is only love and the sharing of knowledge from your body-wisdom to your mind and heart. It is nothing more than acknowledgment that a mind-body relationship exists. Although we will be identifying the many and varied ways your body has been affected by your pattern, we do it with compassion and with the desire to appreciate how thoughts and behaviors impact a close friend.

Negative thought patterns disrupt your body on two levels. One is the vibration of the negative thought pattern itself. The body feels what you think. The second level is the way those thought patterns cause you to behave toward your body regarding, for instance, exercise, sleep, nutrition, and addictions.

The mind-body connection is real. Maintaining balance within the context of this close connection is your body's highest priority and obligation to you, and yours to it. Over time negative messages throw the body off balance. Depending on the strength and constitution of your body, you may be able to get away with negative thought patterns for a long time before the body says – *I can't do this any longer.*

If awareness does not happen in time to stop the cause and resulting effect, then the body gets sick.

If ever you've had a good friend who is able to listen to you without judgment, and who reflects back what has been said with kindness and presence, you know how validating and nurturing this alone can feel. That is all we are doing in this Discovery Prompt. We are merely listening and acknowledging what the body has to say. More simply still, all I will be asking you to do here is to name any and every health issue you have ever hoped to improve. This could be something as simple as brittle nails or as complex as a life-threatening health condition. If it is body related, it belongs here.

So far, I have asked you to stay on topic in order to keep your clearing work streamlined all the way through the prompts, however, here feel free to list as many physical conditions as you can think of, even if you aren't sure it relates to your pattern. Your body is subjected to every pattern, so here it all counts. You will not be perpetuating an already existing condition by honoring your body for how it is impacted by your thoughts and actions. Your intention is to give your body acknowledgment and understanding, and because it is in context of a larger pattern at work, you will be giving your body comfort and relief.

Some examples to get you started might be dehydration, insomnia, sleep apnea, panic attacks, back pain, frequent colds, near or farsightedness, headaches, baldness, grey hair, carpal tunnel syndrome, food allergies, hip pain, athlete's feet, parasites, varicose veins, dry skin, cataracts, weight gain, weight loss, thinning hair, shingles, cancer, candida, viruses, aging, neck pain, nail biting, addictions, eczema, bursitis, knee pain, sexual issues, diabetes, broken bones, lack of flexibility, cavities, root canals, joint pain, heart attacks, bug bites, etc.

Even if it is not a current issue, yet used to be an issue, go ahead and list it. Any physical condition simple or complex, current or in the past, common or unusual, is welcome to be acknowledged here. Scan your body as you think of your pattern and see what jumps into your awareness. Remember this writing is for your eyes only. No one ever has to see it.

Clearing patterns is like following breadcrumbs in a forest. Many of these breadcrumbs were left there for you by your inner child and your body memory. You'll always get to where you need to go if only you listen carefully to yourself and follow your own good sense. The wonderful part is, the more patterns you clear, the more good sense you will have. Your good sense has been there all along. It's just that now you will be far more aware of it and able to more deeply trust it.

Call in the presence of divine love, your higher self and soul and let's begin.

Your Journaling Prompt:

Here you give time and energy, thought and love, to acknowledge how your beloved body has been compensating for, and has been affected by, your thoughts and actions. Name your physical conditions, as many as you can think of, current or in the past, to fully honor your body. If you've experienced a physical condition and feel it might be related to your pattern, or even if you aren't sure, it doesn't matter, write it down. You may find yourself saying – *Oh, this is why* _____.

No physical condition is too complex or too trite. It all counts here. By naming it you are giving yourself a chance to find balance and a new level of health. Acknowledgment is honoring, and by honoring we bring love. There is no judgment about health conditions.

There is only love, acceptance, acknowledgment and a willingness to bring attention to what has been.

How many to name? Write down as many as you can. Fifty is not too many. Ten is not too few. We all have something. Breathe in a huge dose of self-love and acceptance, and let the honoring begin.

Wonderful work. Your body loves you. It lives for you. You cannot be here without it. Whatever you can do to love and support your body will come back to you with good health and lotus flower joy. Your body is your sacred sanctuary and what you just accomplished brought honor to your physical, living home. Your body is holy ground, and it thanks you for acknowledging it. I humbly bow to your efforts and stand witness to your desire to live free, healthy and full of life.

Please stay with me as we address your pattern's habits, obsessions and compulsions in Discovery Prompt 8.

Chapter Twenty: Discovery Prompt 8
Recognize Your Habits, Obsessions and Compulsions

Bad habits get established when we ignore how we feel the first time or two we engage in them. Let's say we overeat something that doesn't agree with us and we get a stomachache, or we drink too much and get a hangover, or we try a cigarette once and it makes us cough. It makes sense to stop ingesting that substance. We didn't like it, so we stopped or modified the behavior. Or, let's say someone is abusive to us and we set a strong boundary with him or her to stop that behavior. This is a sign of our own well-being at work. It's natural to look out for our own best interests. We should. That's our job.

Now let's say we engage in a behavior which feels awful, but yet we do not stop the behavior. Instead, we override our feelings and do it again anyway. Maybe it feels less awful the next time, and after a few more attempts, the once awful behavior starts to feel more normal. We've adjusted to it. This is how a new norm gets established for well-being.

Now something awful somehow feels okay. Once this happens, we can't remember what true well-being felt like. This is one way in which negative habit patterns get started, and this can be true for many kinds of compulsions, including our inner dialogue – the way we talk to ourselves.

Our goal in this Discovery Prompt is to bring you back to balance and true well-being by acknowledging the habits and compulsions that feed into your pattern. In the scope of this journaling practice, a habit or compulsion is any thought or behavior we engage in to numb the emotional pain of a negative truth we feel we just can't face. Habits and compulsions take many forms and all patterns have them.

We could also use the word *addiction* here. The word addiction calls to mind behaviors like substance abuse, yet we can also become habituated to repetitive thought patterns as well: jealousy, envy, hatred, sulking, complaining, obsessing about one's weight, etc. And we can become addicted to other people. A codependent behavior, such as obsessing about whether or not someone else approves of you, or is in love with you, falls into this category.

It's okay to be creative and to use the word habits and addictions differently than how you would normally think of them. There's magic in this. It levels the playing field. Everyone has habits, compulsions and addictions to some degree; these thoughts and behaviors can run a wide spectrum. Some are more poisonous than others, for sure, yet patterns use obsessive habits to distract us. They just do. Calling obsessive habits *addictions* helps the mind take notice, but it doesn't really matter what you call them.

There's no judgment about our pattern's habits and compulsions, and if these words don't quite fit for you, call it a sabotage-tendency, or an escapism-route, or think of it as a behavior, that up until now, you have not been able to stop. Dependency is another appropriate term here. Use whatever word or phrase you wish as long as it doesn't excuse the habit. All we are doing is making the habit conscious so you can clear your pattern. Nothing more. You will know you have cleared your pattern successfully when your urge to engage in a certain obsessive behavior has either stopped or has been lessened, or if you find yourself thinking about it differently.

Trying to stop a habit can elicit strong emotional reactions regardless of type or severity. Our habits don't like to be threatened. Naming habits might cause you to experience intense emotions. If this happens, just breathe and let your emotions pass through you. Stay grounded. There is no judgment here. We don't want to upset any compulsions and get them going. We just want to bring balance to the issue you are addressing.

It can be difficult to understand the obsessive, blinding, rigid, conniving, sneaky, seductive ways of a habit if you have never tried to overcome one. Habits and addictions can be illusionary on their own, without the help of a larger pattern at work. And more often than not, there is a larger pattern at work, and generally the habit is itself a symptom or a coping mechanism of that larger pattern.

In this step, you detach further and become more objective and ask what behaviors relate to your pattern that could be considered seductive and deceptive? There will likely be an element of shame mixed in with the behavior – *Whenever I think* _____ *I make myself feel better by doing* _____.

Again, the ability to identify a feeling and trace the feeling back to original thought is essential. Yet, even if the skill of identifying thoughts and feelings is new to you, that's okay. It won't be for long. You will get good at this.

It may be you have already overcome a previous addiction and, if so, then you will have a good sense of how seductive and sneaky this energy can be. If, in fact, you have already overcome a previous addiction, then I'd like to point out that you have likely already cleared many patterns. Otherwise, you could not have overcome it. If you are currently working a program around a specific addiction and feel that you still have to use a lot of willpower in order to stick to your program, then this spiritual practice can help you go to the next level of peace and commitment to your program.

Furthermore, if you've cleared one addiction, you will be able to clear other addictions. We clear patterns and addictions one thought at a time, one Discovery Prompt at a time. Addictions use tricky thinking to fool us, but we have a method that is far trickier. We have a spiritual practice that uses every angle of attack. If you approach this with an open, honest heart, and I trust you will, no addiction will still be left unaddressed when we are done.

Remind yourself you are not your habits, compulsions or addictions. These thoughts and behaviors are just strategies that patterns use to perpetuate a cycle of pain and only because they don't have a better idea. The pattern message of an addiction will promise you comfort and relief, but instead will cause some kind of further setback. What behaviors can you name that deliver a different result than what you think you will get? When your pattern is activated, what appears to offer you relief? What kind of self-defeating behavior does your pattern cause you to do? How do you feel after you do it? What does it tell you to expect? What does it actually deliver?

You may notice you are conscious enough to identify your thoughts when they hit, but you'll have the tendency to engage in the behavior anyway. A telltale sign is that an addiction makes a harmful, toxic behavior seem exciting, thrilling and enjoyable, and your pattern tells you it is okay to do it. It tells you it will be different this time. This time will feel like the first time. In truth, though, the pain the behavior causes is worse than the pain it is trying to numb. What behaviors have you tried to stop in the past but could not overcome? What actions do you deny or defend?

When someone else enables our habits, it is called codependency. Some habits and addictions are more difficult to spot when someone else is taking the hit for us, preventing us from feeling the full effect of our behavior. If someone makes excuses for your habit or joins you in defending it, it's like *cause and effect* with the *effect* once removed. When the effects of our actions are buffered or encouraged or defended, it takes us longer to figure them out. If others enable your behavior, you may have to look deep for the habits and addictions your pattern typically uses.

Further, if the folks you hang out with have the same habit you have, you will be swimming in it. You will have to be the smartest fish in the pond to figure it out. And you are, because you're learning how painful emotional energy works, and once you understand how painful energy functions, you can't be outsmarted by it. It can no longer cause you to pretend you don't know any better, or to pretend you are not in pain. You do know better and you are strong enough to face any pain long enough to deal with it once and for all.

When pain energy is running the show, it feels good to hurt. Addictions cause us to go to extremes. According to the urge of an addiction, if a little pain feels good, a lot will feel even better. You'll want to make note of those times when you let yourself succumb to pain in an *it hurts to feel good* sort of way. Your true soul-intelligence doesn't function this way, but harmful addiction patterns do. When we allow pain energy to completely take us over, it often doesn't release us until it has taken us for a full *joy* ride. Then we are left feeling terrible. After effects of a pain-joy ride can be humiliation, defeat, anger, resistance, fear, more denial, confusion and sadness.

Again, you may think creatively about habits here. Anything can be considered a habit, a compulsion or an addiction in this work. If your pattern causes you to talk on the phone too much when you need to be focusing on something else, write it down. Don't worry if you already listed a certain behavior in a previous step. There will be overlap with other steps. That's okay. In fact, we want this. Your mind needs this because when we are able to see the messages that remain and persist, we are able to examine them more deeply.

We all have a collection of bad habits and addictions we carry around comingled with our patterns, so where to start? Identifying the most painful habit first will get you on your way. It will be the easiest to spot. You know what causes you the most pain. That's always the place to start. Addictions tell fascinating stories. Just stay in your heart about it, listening to what your habits and compulsions want you to know about why they cause you to do what you do. Take a deep breath. You are okay no matter what is going on. Stay appropriately detached, notice how these messages feel in your body, and please do write them down.

Your Journaling Prompt:

Take a moment to call in your higher guidance. Love and help are close by. Knowing you are infinitely loved no matter what, and with as much self-compassion as you can muster, name at least 5 to 10 habits, compulsions or addictions by finishing the following statements:

When I am sad, my pattern tells me I will feel better by doing _____.

When my feelings are hurt, the first thing I do is _____.

After a long day at work when I feel depleted, I _____.

When I feel jealous or envious my tendency is to _____.

My pattern causes me to use other people to feel better by _____.

I absolutely cannot stop doing _____.

When I am lonely, I tend to _____.

When I am angry, I tend to _____.

People say I _____ too much.

I avoid certain tasks or I procrastinate by _____.

When I want more excitement, I engage in_____.

What behaviors have you tried to stop in the past, but could not overcome? What actions do you deny or defend? What substances or people have you become overly reliant upon? What behaviors do you think are no big deal and would never dream of giving up?

Think back to how long some of these behaviors have been with you and recall when they first began. Everything has a root, a beginning, and with acknowledgment, will come understanding and awareness.

From a spiritual perspective, you are always loved and respected – your spirit is always safe. There is no judgment about these behaviors. Habits and addictions exist on patterns for good reasons. Here we take heart and we bring love, acceptance and acknowledgment to the ways our patterns cause us to engage in unsustainable behaviors. This is how we set ourselves free and call back our balanced power.

Great job! What you just accomplished took willingness, objectivity, commitment and keen self-observation skills. Not everyone has the focus and patience to do what you just did. I applaud your courage and dedication. Thank you for working so hard on your patterns.

Your time and effort focused on creating inner balance is a gift to the world. It's time for a nice hot cup of tea. You've earned it!

Chapter Twenty-One: Discovery Prompt 9
Give Voice to Your Traumas, Shame, Phobias, and Fear

Our more intense emotional reactions stem from thought patterns that were established during especially difficult or shocking moments. In this Discovery Prompt we remember significant past events that relate to our pattern. I will ask you to *feel* into your current situation and to identify strong and corresponding emotions from the past that relate to your current issue.

When an event occurs faster than you can process the emotional energy it creates, the mind tries to make sense of the event the best it can. In trying to make sense of an event during fight-or-flight moments, negative decisions about oneself or about life in general are established and then those decisions – and stories that result from them – repeat.

Just like in the previous Discovery Prompt, we will be defining trauma in ways that encompass a broader scope than how you might normally think of trauma. Here trauma is defined as anything that shocked you enough to cause you to lock-in a negative belief about yourself. This could be anything.

It could be an event as seemingly insignificant as skinning your knee at age five to a much more serious one such as being emotionally or physically abused. When it comes to shock and trauma, the body doesn't know the difference between real or imagined, and it doesn't matter if the event was emotional or physical.

Being told by your partner he or she is leaving you for another lover is traumatic in a different way than being pursued by a grizzly bear, of course, but both traumas affect the body in similar ways. They both alert the body of danger and thereby make the heart pump faster, suppress the immune system in order to reserve energy needed to defend against the danger, and pump blood to the parts of the body needed to fight or flee the enemy, to name a few.

The body only registers *danger!* It doesn't distinguish whether the threat is physical or emotional, real or imagined. All the body cares about in this scenario is safety. Depending on the sensitivity of your emotional and physical makeup, it might not take much to establish a fight-or-flight reaction to a hurtful event.

After a triggering event has ended, the imprinted message remains in emotional and physical memory and can reinvent itself countless times in other forms, reinforcing the same message with or without variation. These imprints can become a self-fulfilling prophecy whereby a person will unknowingly place themselves in circumstances that repeat the imprinted message, until they address what originally caused the trauma.

These messages live at the subconscious level of your mind, which means they become a part of your free will choices. When we are clearing a pattern, we want to list all the traumas in which the pattern has its rooting. In this Discovery Prompt we identify the string of related traumas that use the same energy theme. We will be listing traumatic themes that reinforce the same beliefs keeping in mind there will likely be several different traumatic themes to trace. This isn't as difficult as it might sound. As long as you can identify your feelings you can do this. It goes like this:

> Realize the beliefs that make up your current issue are rooted in past experience.
>
> Identify the way your current issue feels in your body. Where do you feel it in your body? Do you feel it in your head, heart or gut, or someplace else?
>
> Identify your feelings. I feel _____.
>
> Link your current feelings to past events when you felt this way before, going all the way back to childhood. Ask yourself when and where you remember feeling this exact same way before, continuing to stay focused on how your body feels.

When you get to the Journaling Prompt, you will make notes about what you remember, answering – *What happened? How old were you? Who was involved? What is your memory and how does it relate to your current issue?*

Just as with all the other Discovery Prompts, I suggest that you call on spiritual support to help you recall as many specific thematically related incidents as possible. You will scan the event in your mind and identify the judgments that got established. And, consider what you might have decided about yourself and your life.

For example, I decided life wasn't safe or fair. I decided people don't understand me. I decided I'm smart and everyone else is an idiot. I decided I'm helpless. I decided I have no value. I decided I'm not lovable. I decided to take the blame because no one else could handle the responsibility. I decided they were right about me – I'd never amount to anything. I decided to be lonely, depressed and to go without. I decided I was invisible and there was nothing I could do about it.

You will be looking for a subconscious message here. Listen closely for it.

So, *there is what happened*, and *there is what you decided based on what happened* and then *there is the behavior of how that decision played out*. For example, I decided *no one would ever treat me that way again*, and that's when I became *a bully*, or I decided *I never wanted to be poor* and that's when I became *a workaholic*, or I decided *there wasn't enough to go around* and if I was going to get what I needed, *I would have to hoard the resources*, or I decided *to never let myself need anything from anyone ever again*, and that's when I *became reclusive*.

Keep in mind not all defining events are isolated episodes. Sometimes the trauma was an ongoing chronic abuse, meaning you were continuously immersed in it. If you identify that a traumatic theme on your pattern was a chronic ongoing trauma, rather than a string of separate events, you will need to take extra care to identify it. It is understandably difficult to identify abusive themes when those themes were all you knew at the time. It is further complicated, especially if the abuse is still happening. How do you explain water to a fish? The fish has to want to hear it and has to take a leap of faith to trust the information.

I will occasionally see a client who tells me they have no memory of their childhood. In this case, I encourage them to keep asking questions until something sparks. When we become ready to remember, and we ask the question – *What happened?* – the answer will find its way to us.

Take a moment now to recall your Highest Intention. What is your aim? What is your desire? What does your life look like without this pattern? The comparison and contrast help us to tune into the opposite energy, and to identify the energy we need to clear out.

One way to allow for comparison is to connect to your core spiritual presence, the part of you that always knows best, and then compare the two experiences. Feeling strong, peaceful, respected, cared for and loved feels _____ (soothing, fulfilling, nurturing, safe, warm, joyful). By comparison, emotional and physical mistreatment feels _____ (angering, empty, lonely, disconnected, unsafe, frightening).

The goal of this work is to reset and recalibrate your internal reference point for feeling good. When you experience pain for too long, it's easy to lose your innate and natural ability to feel safe and secure.

How do you name an ongoing trauma that is so familiar you don't know any better, or a deeply buried trauma you do not remember? You can ask – *Was there a trauma I suffered in which I was too immersed to accurately identify, or a trauma that happened which I no longer remember?*

Then sleep on it. Dream about it. Write it out when it shows up. It will. Ask it to show up. Nothing can stay hidden when we ask. When something becomes painful enough, we ask the hard questions and then, in divine right timing, we become ready to hear the answers. That's why they say *you've got to want it* when it comes to healing deeper wounds. It takes focused intention. It takes a sincere desire to heal.

You can also become shocked or traumatized by events to which you didn't give much attention at the time yet something significant about the messaging from the event stayed with you. It could be an event you deemed insignificant, yet it may actually hold more energy for you in regard to your pattern than some of the more obvious incidents. Grant yourself permission to acknowledge how you feel.

In order to thoroughly release the energy that causes a traumatic theme to repeat, you need to list the whole string of related traumatic incidents on that particular theme. For example, if you have an abandonment trauma or a loss trauma, the string of events might look something like this:

Age 11: We moved and left all my friends behind. I felt lost.

Age 12: My girlfriend pretended not to know me when my family went back to visit. I was heartbroken.

Age 17: I was betrayed by my best friend, Joe. I was stunned and heartbroken.

Age 23: My mom died. I felt lost and heartbroken.

Age 29: My new boss didn't believe my story about what happened during that one work incident and betrayed me in front of our entire crew. It was a double trauma: I had the mishap itself to deal with, and the fact that my superior misrepresented me to my peers. I felt shocked, insulted and shamed. I'm still angry.

Only include enough details so you know what you are talking about, and to identify feelings associated with the event so that you can keep moving. Do your best to name as many related traumatic incidents as you can, noting the ones with the most charge on them. Stay present to your body, allowing your body memory to help you. You will likely feel the answers in your gut. The feelings for each trauma imprint will feel the same regardless of the varying incidents.

In the Journaling Prompt, you will be asked to record any insights such as – *No wonder I believe _____. No wonder I drew that conclusion considering what I went through.* Stay on topic with your trauma stream. How will you know you are on topic? You will feel it; and, because you are sincere about clearing your pattern, you will be guided. Trust yourself. You can do this.

The specific ways you were imprinted by certain experiences are unique to your circumstances, personality type, family system, age and culture, etc. All information that comes to you must pass through your own unique worldview filter. Who knows what really happened during some of these events by the time the information makes its way through all these filters?

For example, when a victim filter is strong it will cause you to perceive hurtful incidents as a deliberate attack. You might ask – *How does my pattern convince me I am helpless or powerless in certain situations? What story does it tell me? What does it say that causes me to expect to be swindled, conned, used, sacrificed or exploited?*

Closely related to trauma imprints are the topics of Shame, Phobias and Fear.

Shame is the result of misunderstood traumatic circumstances. It is powerful to list the core traumas that pertain to your pattern but also identify the feelings of shame, humiliation, embarrassment, and demoralization if those feelings were present.

You may find yourself narrowing the feelings down to one core sentence such as – *I notice whenever my pattern causes me to _____, I feel embarrassed.*

Write down how you anticipate your pattern will humiliate you in the future. Fear of a repeat incident mixed with shame and humiliation is fertile soil for pain energy to continue to grow and survive. Calling it out, making it conscious, and letting it go, stops this cycle, especially now, because you are doing it in the context of the entire pattern.

As you are listing the traumatic themes of your pattern, you may find it clarifying to narrow the trauma energy down further to one core fear and one core feeling of shame.

You might write – *My greatest fear on this pattern is _____. My greatest shame is _____.*

Phobias are irrational *fears*. They are the mind's attempt to prevent something bad from happening again. Understanding traumatic events and naming the resulting encoded beliefs is how we clear a phobia. As you list the traumas associated with your pattern, also consider any phobias your pattern might contain. By naming phobias during whole-pattern-clearing work, you give these issues a chance to heal along with the entire pattern in which they are enmeshed.

Compassionately spoken, it is not that bad things are allowed to happen on earth. Rather, it is that things happen, traumas get encoded and then, unless we do something to heal them, they repeat. We have the power to change our patterning. We have free will to be here, to interact, to understand our *soul-contracts* with others, to have things happen, to grow from them, and to heal. It is all a part of our wondrous, magical lives.

Please remember to call in your higher guidance. You are never alone in this work. Please also revisit your original issue to stay on track as contrasted against your Highest Intention to guide your work. Your spirit is always resting peacefully on the lotus flower no matter what is going on. Always you are infinitely loved.

Your Journaling Prompt:

Refer back to Discovery Prompts 3 – 6 as often as necessary to spark ideas about emotional themes, which should also help evoke your emotional memory of related events. Write down what comes to mind using a stream-of-consciousness mind-set. With your Highest Intention in mind, feel your current issue in your body and using your list-prompts from previous Discovery Prompts, think back to when you've felt this way before.

Let your body wisdom remind you of what you need to remember, revisiting past scenes just enough to get the messages that got encoded. Listen deeply to yourself. Feel your feelings. You know these answers because you were physically there when these events happened. It is okay if the messages sound rather juvenile to you. Again, as we learned earlier, messages imprint using the logic of the age you were when the event happened. You are an adult now so you'll have an adult perspective and, of course, you'll have your higher spiritual support to guide you through.

How many traumas to list? Try to identify 1 – 3 different emotional themes containing 3 – 5 specific events per theme, starting with the earliest event you can recall to the most recent, including acknowledging the emotions and decisions you may have made as a result of each theme. Be sure to note associated phobias, the core fear and the core shame.

We are looking for new insights that explain why you believe what you believe in regard to your current issue, as many as you can get.

Your own trusting spirit already knows how to do this. However, it is okay if you need to read this section several times until you grasp it. Just let the words remind you of what you already know how to do.

Go to your neutral place of peace and give your inner child a hug. He or she remembers enough to give you the information you need. What you don't remember will find its way to you in due time. Just do your best. Allow self-compassion to flow into your heart. There is a reason for every belief. Let your desire for greater freedom and joy lead the way. You are not your patterns and you are not limited by any past experience. Your beloved spirit is greater than all of this. You are safe. Life is cheering you on. This is how you transcend your past. You can totally do this. Just go for it!

⚘ ⚘ ⚘

Welcome back. No doubt you have just set free a ton of trapped energy. You are now allowing light to come in through all the cracks, healing the pieces and bringing it all back to wholeness. There is so much love and compassion when showing up for yourself in this way. You are doing it. You are healing your life with this. You are a special, courageous soul to untangle your past in the spirit of your own evolution. Bravo!

Chapter Twenty-Two: Discovery Prompt 10
Explore Your Past (Lives) and Karma

In the Lotus Flower Living Journaling Practice, we use what works. Like me, you may not have been raised to believe in past lives, but if ever you have a tricky pattern you desperately wish to clear, one you can't seem to budge, you might find yourself considering the existence of a central storyline rooted in a previous lifetime.

We all have a past and the past doesn't stay in the past until we address it. For many of us our past is still very present in the form of beliefs, thoughts and behaviors we don't understand.

Many years ago, while considering the evolution of my own soul, and when introduced to the concept of past lives, it made no sense to assume one lifetime, as a white woman, would be enough to give my soul the perspective it needs to fully evolve.

Rather, it resonated with me that one's soul needs many expressions and lifetimes in different bodies with different life themes to fully inform a soul's evolution. So, I adopted this idea and have used it in my own pattern-clearing work since the beginning.

If the idea of past lives does not resonate, you can still do effective clearing work by identifying the archetypal stories in your pattern.

Archetypes are generic human stories and themes that play out across time and across societal contexts. Some common archetypes you might recognize are the hero, the fool, the saboteur, the innocent child, the chosen one, the scapegoat, the bully, the martyr and there are countless others. Archetypes are often the themes of storybooks, poems and movies. Focusing on generic archetypes might not be as intriguing as digging into your past lives, but as long as you can learn what your soul wanted to learn, and you are able to make permanent changes in your behavior, it doesn't matter. Archetypes are discovery tools. They help us to discover our deeper story.

The word *karma* is used in two distinctly different ways in this practice. One is the spiritual law that says – *We reap what we sow*. That is, what we think, believe, and how we act returns to us experiences that match those thoughts, beliefs and actions. In its most concrete essence, you might think of karma as what goes around comes around. This includes our subconscious thoughts and patterning.

The second use of the word karma is the broader concept of past lives, which refers to carryover themes and energies from other lifetimes. This includes past life storylines, which are still playing out in this lifetime because they were not fully understood or overcome or completed in a previous lifetime. The story in this life may have a completely different backdrop, but the main characters will be playing their parts in ways you can recognize. Just as traumas in this lifetime repeat until we process them, past life traumas also continue to repeat until they are fully understood.

Not all current life themes are rooted in past life stories, but you can ask your inner guidance and your angels and guides if your pattern's theme has a deeper root than this lifetime. When we clear out our past life patterning we are essentially addressing the root of the root cause. Once we understand the deepest root cause and harness the gifts and lessons of that lifetime theme, we will finally be free of the effects of that story.

Sometimes a trauma theme will be rooted in several lifetimes. That's when self-compassion really kicks in. When a trauma theme has been carried over several lifetimes, it's no wonder it hurts the way it does.

For additional support, if you are so inclined, there are many great books and audio programs for how to retrieve past life themes. There are also many skilled, intuitive practitioners who can assist you in linking current life patterns to past life patterns.

Whether you approach this step with a past life theme in mind or as a general archetypal storyline, know there are many ways to heal deep wounds and either mind-set can be helpful. What matters most is giving your mind the information it needs to fully detach from a storyline that no longer serves you.

From cultural stereotypes, to archetypes, to past lives, we discover the depth of repeated stories and their impact on our perception, and then change becomes possible, because we understand the root cause. When we can't seem to let go of a certain issue, it is often because we need more information; information that informs and satisfies us from mind, to heart, to soul.

Staying with your originally stated issue, as contrasted against your Highest Intention, call in your spiritual support to protect and guide your work. If you are asking questions, breathing, listening and writing down what you hear, feel and sense you are doing it correctly. Trust yourself, know you are eternally loved, and let's begin.

Your Journaling Prompt:

Whether you know your past life stories or not, this Discovery Prompt can still work for you. If you do not know your past life themes but are open to the possibility of your pattern being rooted in a past lifetime, simply let yourself wonder about it.

What is your innate sense about your pattern's story? Is it a Cinderella theme, a betrayal theme, a fool theme, a self-sabotage theme, a power and control theme, a victim theme?

If you do know your past life story that relates to your pattern, go ahead and jot it down. Evaluate it and see how it relates to your pattern. Note the general theme and the corresponding, supporting beliefs. It will likely match energy for energy the beliefs and feelings you have already captured in previous Discovery Prompts.

A part of you always knows when there is something deeper going on. Self-discovery is about asking probing questions and being willing to receive the answers. Do your best to identify one past life story, or one archetypal theme, that may be playing out in your pattern.

Just like with the other steps, stay objectively neutral and openheartedly detached. There is no judgment on how deeply you might delve into your past. It's all up to you. Either way, you are profoundly loved. Either way, your spirit is still resting with the lotus flower. There is only your story and your desire to bring peace to it. There is only love, safety and infinite support to guide and inspire you on your journey. Just put pen to paper to see what discovery awaits you.

$$\text{❀ ❀ ❀}$$

Welcome back. You are an adventurous spirit. I know this because you are here living on this planet, where the contrasts of experiences are so intense, where truly only adventurers dare tread. As I mentioned in Part I, choosing to find peace in a dimension designed for struggle is a great accomplishment for the soul. Your life themes are fascinating, important and are unique to you. You have choice and you are using your free will to set yourself free. Spectacular work! Now on to Discovery Prompt 11.

* Note: Although I am using the words *past lives*, many people, me included, have welcomed the explanation that perhaps each person's multiple incarnations are all going on simultaneously. We are multidimensional beings, after all. We use the term *past lives* because we exist in linear time where past, present and future mean something to our minds. From a soul perspective, however, the soul does not exist in linear time.

Chapter Twenty-Three: Discovery Prompt 11
Shed Light on Your Pattern's Resentments,
Self-Sabotaging Tendencies and Prideful Opinions

You are so much more than any pattern and certainly you are more than any pattern message. We untangle our pattern's messages down to these particular specifics so our pattern can no longer operate through us in the ways it currently does, so our true spirit can freely express without worry of things going wrong. We do this by shedding light on the predictable ways our pattern causes us to think and behave.

Deeply negative emotions such as resentment, hatred, grudges, jealousy, arrogance and pride are so destructive they warrant their own Discovery Prompt in this process. Toxic emotions like these do double harm. Not only do they perpetuate negative feelings, they cause us to subconsciously betray our own treasured values. Meaning, these particular emotions give us exacting, immediate karmic backlash. For example, if you hate your mother-in-law and you value honesty, the hatred might cause you to lie to her. Or, if you have a good work ethic yet hold a grudge against your boss, the grudge might cause you to deliver poor results. This is because no matter how well-intentioned we are, if we harbor bitter feelings, those feelings find ways to express themselves.

At times these emotions are so deep, we may not be conscious of how they cause us to behave. Anger, resentment, hatred and grudges can be so blinding we might act aggressively and then be shocked by other people's responses, thinking *they* started it. Even in situations where we feel our resentment is justified, bitter feelings work against us.

Sometimes our bitter judgments about other people are unfounded. There are times a pattern message is so deeply grooved in our psyche, it may cause us to project and perceive a behavior from another that didn't actually even occur. Unwittingly, we walk away convinced our perception was accurate. When honestly, our pattern was projecting a false picture of reality it has created many times before.

Other times, an insult did occur but was exaggerated by our mind. Someone may have said something hurtful, yet our pattern caused us to elaborate, inflate and dramatize what we heard. The very fact we believed it is another clue there's more to understand and to clear out. You may find your mind in argument about it, defending your view that the other person's words were meant as an intentional, personal attack on you, whether they were or not.

In some instances, hatred is rooted in feelings of envy. Envy is a reaction to the belief *there is not enough for me*. As in, *there's only one of that and he has it; therefore, I can't have it*. In a world of unlimited possibilities, however, someone else having something is merely evidence you can have it, too. Envy then is nothing more than a clue that you're seeing something you'd like to have. If they have it then you can have it, too, or some better version that's tailored just for you.

You might observe you don't *always* harbor these emotions. It may be you only experience them when your pattern is triggered, as this is often the case.

Another way to think about intense emotions such as hatred, envy and resentment is as a *self-sabotage* tendency. It is like the idiom that says – *Your lack of forgiveness hurts you more than it hurts them.* These poisonous emotions cause us to work against our own best efforts.

A sabotage tendency is an act of self-betrayal that causes you to ruin a project just before it's finished, or to spend too much money on clothes when you are trying to save for school. It might cause you to gain back the five pounds you just lost. It might cause you to exaggerate or to lie. It might cause you to end a relationship that was actually good for you. There may be a strong urge to act poorly, and to feel as though you have no choice in the matter. It may cause you to seduce others with your charm, or to be seduced by someone else's charm. Yet no one can seduce us unless we leave a doorway open in our own energy field, inviting it in with our own sabotage patterns.

Another aspect of the snarled web of *resentment, envy* and *self-sabotaging* tendencies is the way these emotions arouse our egoic pride to action. Whether I am clearing a pattern on myself or assisting another with their pattern, I ask about the ways the pattern evokes a sense of exaggerated pride or arrogance. How does the pattern cause you to act conceited, put on airs, feel superior, or defend your importance or value?

For example, when activated our pattern may inadvertently cause us to act boastful, exaggerate our talents, or to take credit for things we did not do, or to put others down in an effort to feel superior to them. A part of you might say – *No, I don't do any of these things.* And, at the heart of your true nature you probably do not consciously do these things, yet patterns cause us to unconsciously do or think these things. In this prompt, we call it out. We know it is not our true nature. It is just a predictable pattern behavior.

Understandably, most of us don't want to admit what our patterns cause us to do, so in this Discovery Prompt it might be helpful to bring in a sense of humor. Step into your expanded, light-filled self and let yourself be amused as you evaluate this aspect of your pattern. You might even just start by guessing. You might wonder – *If I were to entertain this idea that my pattern causes me to be arrogant, what is my guess about what it causes me to do?* For example, how does your pattern justify its existence? Does it tell you, you are smarter, superior, special or unique in an exaggerated, *I am right and they are wrong* kind of way?

Arrogant messages may very well be based on true strengths, but they will be embellished. It might be true you are effective at your job, yet the pattern's message will assert you are the best at it, everyone else is a moron, and how dare they not recognize this fact.

It might be helpful to finish the following statements:

I am the smartest at _____.

I am better at _____ than anyone else I know.

I am the only one who can _____.

Arrogances will sound like absolute statements of fact, and they will reoccur whenever your issue is activated. Don't be concerned if they are true, not true or partially true or whether or not you consistently do or don't express these emotions. If you hear, feel or somehow sense them, get them down because they hold energy. The moment you write them down, you will know what is true and not true. Also, you do not need to list all the arrogant opinions you've ever caught yourself thinking. Only list the ones that directly pertain to the current issue. It's okay if there is overlap with other steps.

Always, at your core, you are a loving, flexible spirit who only wants to be and do the best you can with the life you are living. Always, you are stronger, wiser and more resilient than any of your pattern's emotional expressions. These emotions are likely only showing themselves in very specific contexts when your pattern has been triggered. This is how we turn off the activation switch.

Your Journaling Prompt:

With lightness of heart, and knowing these are nothing more than predictable, common pattern strategies, give yourself the relief of admitting any *resentments*, *hatreds*, *bitterness*, *grudges* or feelings of *envy* or *jealousy* which may be hidden in your pattern. Who or what do you resent? Who or what does your pattern cause you to hate? Against whom do you harbor feelings of envy? Who or what can't you forgive? What evokes in you feelings of bitterness and how does it express? At the level of your pattern's messaging, how do you hear, feel or experience it?

Can you further identify how your pattern's resentments cause you to sabotage your own best efforts? Can you name scenarios of how your emotions cause karmic backlash? What happens? How do you step on your own toes? Does your pattern cause you to say or do things that go against your own values? What do you value and how does your pattern cause you to behave contrary to those values? What are you thinking right before you have the urge to act poorly? What is the message? What is the behavior?

How or what does your pattern cause you to misperceive? Do you go unconscious during the behavior? What can you glean from how other people respond to your behavior?

What are your strong prideful opinions and arrogances in regard to your pattern? What are your exaggerated strengths? What does your pattern tell you to help you feel superior to others or above it all?

Just write one word at a time as you hear it, without any judgment. Let your pattern talk. Staying in your neutral, objective mind-set, give these feelings and behaviors their moment to be witnessed. This is how we take the charge off. With a compassionate smile and a lighthearted focus, enjoy a sense of comic relief as you sit in the audience of your pattern's theatre noting its resentments, sabotage tendencies and prideful opinions.

You are none of these feelings or behaviors. You are a spiritual being expressing a human life, with a personality, living in a sea of family and cultural messages, countless recurring experiences, carrying pattern behaviors that once you know what you are looking for, are easier to spot.

Notice where you feel these emotions in your body and please do write them down.

Welcome back. You just released a lot of trapped energy. Can you feel the difference? You are not a resentful, self-sabotaging, arrogant person. You are a lighthearted, thoughtful, caring, loving spirit with human patterning that we are now untangling piece by piece. Furthermore, you have impeccable timing. You have chosen to live on the planet now when the environment is ultra-supportive of doing all kinds of inner transformational work. In this, your willingness to ask the deeper questions will take you far. Brilliant job! Well done!

Chapter Twenty-Four: Discovery Prompt 12
Reveal Your Pattern's Threats and Intimidation

Every pattern has within it a bully, a threatening voice, which tries to prevent you from evolving beyond its influence. It pretends to protect you. It does this by sending any number of scary messages that essentially say – *If you clear this pattern, you will be sorry. You need me. If you change the status quo, bad things will happen.* This voice tries to convince you it is being helpful, when in truth it is perpetuating an experience you no longer wish to have.

This fear-based, intimidating voice speaks up anytime we step forward to stop a pattern of behavior. It is the voice that says – *No, do not change the way you are doing things. This is working.* Often this voice sounds real and convincing. Meanwhile, you know better. The only reason it has had any leverage up until now is because it is likely somewhat unconscious and half muted. Make no mistake though; it is powerful and is worth the effort to bring your attention to this voice to call it out for what it is.

In this Discovery Prompt we confront this threatening voice. We make its false threats loudly conscious so you can make a new decision about to whom and to what you should listen. We identify the specific threats it makes. Then we can know if the resulting, unconscious fear we feel is warranted or not. Usually, it is not. But how can we know if we don't take a moment to expose the lightning fast messages it sends?

Depending on your pattern, the message will be – *Without me, you will be _____ (lonely, poor, sick, unlovable, bullied, rejected, humiliated, disrespected, unsafe, found out, ugly, killed, etc.).* The message will sound exaggerated and dramatic, and you will likely feel its impact at the body level as a real threat.

Although you may not have been aware of this voice until now, I have yet to sit with a client who could not name these messages once they understood what I was asking them to do. You know this voice. It is the voice that makes you doubt you can or should change. It makes you question whether or not it is safe to change. It intimidates you into thinking it is better to live with your current mind-set than to try and risk living without it.

Here are some examples to get you started:

> I can't give up this stagnant love relationship because I hear the message – *It is this or nothing.* The threat is loneliness.

> I can't leave my dead-end job because I hear the message – *If you go after your dream career, you won't have any money.* The threat is financial stability.

> If I stop my overeating pattern, and lose weight, *I might be more attractive to potential dating partners.* The threat is vulnerability.

> I can't stop smoking because if I do, *I will lose my smoke-break friends.* The threat is abandonment.

> I can't stop my worry habit because *worrying keeps me alert for potential disasters.* The threat is safety.

> I can't give up drinking because *when I drink, I am the life of the party.* The threat is losing a sense of camaraderie.

> I can't give up my fear of public speaking because *I am terrified I will embarrass myself in front of a group of people.* The threat is humiliation.

Only you know the ways your pattern threatens you. These threats will be unique to your specific pattern. However, I will offer that loneliness, poverty, humiliation, safety, loss of health and even death are common threats.

Worth noting: By clearing your threats, you will NOT be opening yourself up to danger. Quite the opposite is true; you will be preventing a self-fulfilling prophecy from happening. In fact, you may already be experiencing self-fulfilling results from these threatening messages. You might ask – *Is this message protecting me, or is it actually causing what I fear? What is the threat? What am I actually experiencing?*

As with other steps, let yourself feel the feelings of the threat. You can trust your logical, soulful self to discern the difference between an empty threat and a functional thought. As soon as you have the threat in your grasp, work to slip back into your grounded and logical consciousness. Naming the threat is enough to expose its false nature. You will know you have named a threat correctly when you find yourself taking a spontaneous, deep breath.

Living a lotus flower life, feeling connected to the pure, dependable, loving guidance of your sweet soul is a completely different experience than being pushed around by a lower-vibrational threatening voice. Take a moment to recall your original issue in Discovery Prompt 1 and contrast it against your Highest Intention in Discovery Prompt 2. Your Highest Intention is where you are headed. It is your birthright; and once you are done with this prompt you will be so much closer to it.

Call in your higher support to guide and protect your efforts. Remember you are not your patterns. You are much more than any threatening pattern message. You are strong, focused, clear and determined and there may come a time when you will be able to do this prompt in five minutes or less. Today we don't care how long it takes. We just applaud that you are doing it.

Your Journaling Prompt:

What terrible things does your pattern say will happen if you evolve past its influence? When you get determined to change a behavior, how does your pattern react? What does it tell you will happen? How does it threaten you? How does it scare you into buying into the status quo? What does it say you will lose? How does it say it is protecting you, and what does it actually deliver?

As you think about your current issue as stated in Discovery Prompt 1, and compare it to your Highest Intention in Discovery Prompt 2, what messages try to convince you that you can't have or shouldn't have what you want? What are the threats? With loving detachment and no judgment, just write what you hear exactly as you hear it.

Allow yourself to name at least 6 – 8 threats, or more if you can do so. Note how the threat feels in your body, compare it to your actual experience and remember to breathe. If you hear it in a mean, exaggerated, scary voice, write it down that same way. Name it fully. What do you hear, feel or sense?

Wonderful work! Your pattern can no longer scare you at an unconscious level. You just gave your soul-logic a fighting chance to win this battle. You have made a huge stride toward freedom. You have deflated the energy of your pattern's false threats. This is how you let the light in. This is how you achieve lotus flower peace. You are doing it!

Now let us consider the polar opposite of threats, as we move on to expose your pattern's false benefits.

Chapter Twenty-Five: Discovery Prompt 13
Expose Your Pattern's False Benefits

The title of this Discovery Prompt breaks down into *false*, meaning *not true,* and *benefits* meaning *positive advantage*. Essentially, your pattern's false benefits offer *no true positive advantage*. Yet this is not obvious to the casual observer until time is taken to tune in and expose these messages to your logical mind.

Just as every pattern has within it a bully, every pattern also has an equally convincing voice that says your current way of thinking is benefitting you. While the first voice is threatening you, this voice says do not change this pattern because if you do, you will lose important assets.

The function of your pattern's false benefits is to give you the sense it is what makes you confident, clever, smart, strong, secure, funny, lovable, or any other trait that offers comfort, ease and well-being. It is counting on you to miss the fact that real benefit is not being given.

Just as with threats, these false benefits are not fully conscious to us. They are just conscious enough to confuse us and keep us working in circles. You will know these messages once you bring your attention to them. They are also not necessarily believable and yet, because they are not conscious, we let them have power.

In this Discovery Prompt, you will identify the distorted, positive claims of your pattern. You will give each message a moment to be fully expressed.

You will make them conscious and give your mind a chance to compare what is being communicated versus your real-life experience.

In the following examples, I purposely flipped the messages used in the previous Discovery Prompt so you can see the way a pattern keeps you coming and going in a vicious circle:

I can't give up this stagnant love relationship because my pattern says without it I will have no love at all. The benefit is love.

I can't leave my current job because my dream career doesn't pay enough. The benefit is a higher income.

I can't give up overeating because I won't get enough nutrition. The benefit is nutrition.

I can't give up my smoking habit because if I do I will lose my smoke-break friends. The benefit is friends.

I can't give up my worry habit because worrying keeps me prepared for anything that might happen. The benefit is safety.

I can't stop drinking because when I drink I feel confident and I make friends. The benefit is a sense of belonging.

I can't face my fear of public speaking because I am afraid of being embarrassed. The benefit is emotional safety.

Threats and benefits work hand in hand, and while you may find it easier to identify one or the other, your pattern will use both threats and benefits to prevent you from clearing it. Therefore, it is worth your while to identify both.

Unlike these varied examples, your false benefits will all be related to one pattern, so do your best to keep your focus on the specific pattern you are addressing. Think back to Discovery Prompt 1, the loudest issue in your life, as contrasted to Discovery Prompt 2, your Highest Intention of what life can be like once this issue is fully resolved.

Take a deep, calming breath, as you think about your pattern, meanwhile holding in your heart how you most want to be in the world – free of false promises, full of ease and in love with your life. Call in your spiritual support, and remember your divine spirit is always resting in peace, fully connected and knows the difference between what is real and what is false. Rational, lasting clarity is on its way.

Your Journaling Prompt:

Whenever you get to the place where you say this is it, I have to change, what do you hear your pattern say under the guise of benefits? How does it convince you that staying the same is offering important assets? Whenever you dare evolve beyond your pattern, what false, positive qualities does it say you will lose?

Think about the messages you hear, and the contrary results you often get, as you listen deeply to how your pattern pretends to benefit you. These are not messages that come from your logical mind. They are messages that are generated at the level of your pattern. Don't expect them to make logical sense, but do find them. They are there.

Identify and write down 6 – 8 benefits, or more if you can. You may notice identifying benefits helps you think of more threats. If so, you are doing it correctly. Your pattern is talking to you, which is what we want it to do.

There is no judgment here. There is only awareness and the opportunity to let new understanding have a fighting chance.

Be sure to notice where you feel these messages in your body and please do write them down.

Congratulations! Wow, look how aware you are becoming. Look at how much you have learned. Awareness is how we clear patterns. You are waking up one Discovery Prompt at a time. You are releasing false voices and allowing your loving soul presence to drop in more fully, revealing your lotus flower potential that has been waiting there for you all along. Wonderful work!

Chapter Twenty-Six: Discovery Prompt 14
Untangle Your Pattern's Indecision Loops

We turn our attention now to the aspect of your pattern that is likely causing the biggest energy drain of all: *indecision*. This is the aspect of your issue that presents itself as an impossible dilemma. It often feels like a puzzle you do not know how to solve. It may feel like you are damned if you do, and damned if you don't. This will be an area of life that relates to your pattern where you feel truly stuck.

Earlier in this book, I shared that learning how to stop *the struggle* in a dimension *designed for struggle* is a great accomplishment for the soul. It is also true to say untangling your pattern's indecision loops is a great accomplishment for your mind and heart.

Up until now, when you feel stressed about your pattern, you are likely thinking of your issue with only one side of your brain at a time. We all do this, and for good reasons. This has to do with how the brain is set up to function. Additionally, these thoughts often occur when your attention is divided – meaning, you are only giving it semi-conscious time and devotion. In this Discovery Prompt we take this all into consideration.

The left side of the brain likes to be literal, concrete and logical. The right side of the brain is open, expansive and creative. For example, if you are thinking of your issue while driving and listening to music, you will be evaluating your issue with your right brain. However, if you are pondering your issue while paying bills and doing calculations, you will be evaluating your issue with your left brain.

The untangling magic happens when you put both sides of the dilemma down on paper in one place. This is not like writing the pros and cons of an issue. It can be, but this is more like allowing each side of an argument to have its moment to fully express. Then you can see both opposing frames of logic side by side, each with its special merits and faults. You can see the way they are related, or more clearly just how they are opposed.

Both sides of the dilemma will have their justifications. Both will have exaggerated messages and both will have messages of truth.

While I am using the word indecision, this *energy-knot* in your pattern might not be a decision you need to make, but rather a component of your pattern that feeds confusion. It might be a *moral dilemma*; or, it might be a *relationship* issue; or, it might be a *spiritual* topic you haven't been able to reconcile. It is likely an area of life where it feels like a double bind, a catch-22 or a total conundrum.

Common indecision loops are situations where, for example, it seems time to leave a love relationship but a dependency has developed, as in – *I really want to leave this relationship but I don't know how I will support myself and my kids without it.* Or, perhaps you feel stuck in a dead-end job, the commute is long, and it doesn't pay very well but you don't know what else is out there for you, so you vacillate between doing what you know and taking a huge creative risk. It could be any topic but it will very closely relate to the pattern you are addressing and it will feel like there is no easy solution.

In truth though, there is a solution and it will be close at hand once you see both sides of your indecision loop laid out on paper. Hopefully you have been writing as you go through these prompts. Here it is especially helpful to get it down in written form so you can see and honor both sides of your brain and the way it talks to you.

At last, today is a whole-brain day. Taking this moment to express both sides of your pattern's indecision loops will free your mind and heart of this quandary. Your beautiful soul-logic is waiting for the chance to deliver the peace and clarity that has been there all along.

Your spiritual support and guidance are here and ready. The openness and innocence of your inner child is here, too. Thank yourself for being the receptive and brave person you are, and let's begin.

Your Journaling Prompt:

Remembering this writing is for your eyes only, and you cannot possibly do this wrong, think of the conflict you wrestle with as you *feel* into your pattern. Working on one indecision loop at a time, what particular facet seems irreconcilable? How do you hear it? Write one thought at a time until you have them all on the page.

When you think of your pattern, what particular themes cause your mind to get caught up in a whirling ball of confusion? What specific dilemmas do you find yourself contemplating? You might investigate…

When it comes to my issue:

I am most perplexed by _____.

I cannot seem to reconcile _____.

I can't make sense of _____.

I don't know what to do about _____.

I go back and forth in an endless loop of not knowing how to solve _____.

I hear _____ and then immediately hear the opposing argument of _____.

Keep breathing and do your best to identify 5 – 10 indecision loops in regard to your pattern. All you need to do is put words to both sides of each dilemma to the best of your ability. Your mind and spirit will do their part to untangle it. If you are breathing and feeling as you write, you are doing it correctly. This is your chance to let it out. This is your time. Tell your truth. No matter what it is.

Welcome back! How wonderful to finally have pen and paper at hand to stop the energy drain once and for all. You did it. Now these messages can no longer cycle in your mind. You set them free. You gave them their moment to say what they needed to say. The quiet and harmony you just achieved is yours to keep. The insights you gained have now replaced the indecision loops energy for energy. Congratulations!

You will feel even better and more energy will shift as we turn to Discovery Prompt 15, Clear the Energy.

Chapter Twenty-Seven: Discovery Prompt 15
Clear the Energy

Whether you realize it or not you have been clearing energy all the way through these Discovery Prompts. If you have worked the prompts sincerely and I'm sure you have, then by now you likely already have a very good sense of what has been going on at the level of your pattern's thinking and all that was contributing to that thinking.

Once you've made an entire pattern conscious, the pattern can never impact you the same way again. The insights you have gained can't ever be taken away from you. You worked hard for those insights. They are yours now.

However, since this particular feeling of freedom is a new experience, just for good measure, what follows are statements of release to clear any residual debris of energy that might be lingering. All you need to do here is read, breathe deeply and feel the truth of these statements.

This Discovery Prompt and the one that follows are your big energy paybacks for all your hard work. So please take your time. Go slowly here. There may be statements you will want to read several times to let them settle in for you. Linger on each statement as long as you need, perhaps close your eyes, and really feel it.

To make it more specific and personal, there is a journaling prompt to include any particularly poignant messages that stood out to you in the journaling prompts that came before.

Your higher spiritual support surrounds you now as you do this deep, thorough clearing out of old beliefs and patterning. Knowing more than ever you are not your patterns and you never have been, here you will deliberately release the energy of your pattern once and for all.

Your Journaling Prompt:

If you have worked the Discovery Prompts straight through in one sitting, the messages with the most emotional charge will still be fresh, and in this case, they will likely pop into your mind to be released as you read the release statements.

If you have been working the Discovery Prompts intermittently but still managed to stay on target with your original pattern, then take a moment to look back through your writing to recall any specific messages, habits, behaviors, or beliefs you would like to name and release. Include as many specific aspects you would like to add and speak them at any time during this final purge.

Your words have power. Your clear intention has power. Your desire to be free of this pattern is itself powerful. Claim your innate power to choose to live the life you wish to live. Read the following statements, knowing each statement is real. Also, know that by the power of your word, and in the presence of your higher support, the energy is being released.

Please say with me…

> I now allow any and all lingering traces of negative energy associated with this issue to be fully and completely released, knowing I get to keep what was good and am only releasing that which no longer serves me.

> I now fully and completely release all the limiting beliefs and hiding strategies of this pattern.

> I now fully and completely release the family and cultural messages that no longer serve me in regard to this issue.

> I forgive myself and everyone else who contributed to this issue. We are all free.

I thank my body wisdom for its assistance with this work and I am grateful for all it has done to help me compensate for these limiting messages.

I now claim that all associated physical conditions are harmonized and/or completely healed. My body is free of this entire pattern, and so am I.

I fully accept all gifts gained from the addictions of this pattern and I now fully and completely harmonize, upgrade, integrate and/or release as appropriate all addictions. I forgive all of it.

I fully accept all gifts gained from my past traumatic circumstances and I now fully and completely harmonize, upgrade, integrate and release all negative energy associated with those circumstances from this, and past lives.

I am now free of the energy of any grievances, self-sabotage habits and exaggerated prideful opinions in regard to this issue.

I now claim that all personality traits and compensating strategies are upgraded and harmonized.

I now disprove and release all the supposed benefits and advantages this pattern falsely promised me.

I now discredit and release all the threats and intimidation strategies this pattern falsely used to frighten me.

I now fully release the indecision loops and supposed dilemmas of this pattern, and gratefully accept all the wisdom I derived from them.

My life is now greatly improved by my own effort. Tomorrow when I wake up, after my mind and heart have had a chance to reconfigure themselves, my life will be different and better. I accept lotus flower peace and joy. I am free. I am free. I am free. I feel it. I believe it. I know it. And, so it is….

Magnificent! You have healed your life in a very significant way. You have undeniably exposed the workings of your pattern in its entirety. You stayed with yourself, and with your process, and you have succeeded. You have shifted the energy. You have changed your patterning. You have increased your frequency. You have given yourself and those who love you and the entire world a tremendous gift. Thank you and congratulations!

There is one final action to securely anchor the joy and freedom you have achieved. Please join me in Chapter Twenty-Eight to Declare Your New Truth.

Chapter Twenty-Eight: Discovery Prompt 16
Declare Your New Truth

What is the truth now? Answering this question will have valuable, lasting effects. It will give you more insight into the pattern you just cleared. It will secure the new truth and welcome in the new energy of that truth. Best of all, it will prove to you that you actually did clear your pattern because otherwise you would not be able to answer this question.

All throughout these Discovery Prompts you have been using the expanded, freeing feeling of your Highest Intention to shine light on the darker aspects of your issue and to contrast that feeling against your issue. Meanwhile you have been clearing out the old energy and incrementally bringing in new light and energy. Here you will fully call in that light, energy and information by naming it, as in – *My honest to goodness truth now is* _____.

Your mind and heart need to know exactly how your perception has shifted in order to fully appreciate that your perception has actually changed. So, in this final prompt you will acknowledge your new awareness about your freshly cleared issue. Referring back to your originally stated issue, you will ask questions that are aimed directly at the original issue.

For example, if you worked the Discovery Prompts for raising your sense of self-worth, you would ask – *How do I feel about myself now? How will I treat myself differently now?*

You might write – *The truth is I am valuable no matter who else approves or disapproves of me. The truth is I love myself. The truth is I am peaceful now. The truth is more people love me than I realized.*

If you worked the Discovery Prompts for a pattern around overeating, you might ask – *What's the truth about my eating behavior now? How will my behavior be different now, and why? What did I discover that will help me to be more conscious around food?*

If you worked the Discovery Prompts for accepting more love into your life you might ask – *How do I feel about receiving more love into my life now? What's different? What do I know now about why I couldn't receive love in the past? What surprised me about what I discovered?*

If you worked the Discovery Prompts around a specific phobia you would ask – *How do I feel about this phobia now?* If it was a fear of flying, for example, you might imagine yourself getting on an airplane and ask yourself how that image feels to you now. Does it seem possible for you to get on an airplane and not feel frightened? If so, write about how amazing that feels to you. What's the truth now?

It helps to answer the question – *What did I learn?* I learned _____. You may be able to get 10 new insights out of this question alone. It also helps to answer the question – *What's new?*

My life will be different now because _____.

What most surprised me was _____.

The personality traits I was able to harmonize and now appreciate more are _____.

The prideful opinions I changed were _____.

It may give you more insights to finish the statement:

It's no wonder I had this issue because _____.

I find it feels wonderful to write the truth after a pattern has been cleared. Finishing the statement – *The truth is* _____, may be your longest list of all and, if so, that would be great.

The Truth is all is well.

The Truth is I am always loved.

The Truth is I am always safe.

The Truth is I am lovable and worthy.

The Truth is there is nothing to fear.

The Truth is it is possible to shift my perception.

The truth is there is a deeper reason for everything and now I know how to discover the deeper truth of what motivates me, I can create whatever I wish from a place of balance and love.

That's the truth.

After you write your new truths, I will ask you to choose the ones that make your heart sing the most. There will be some that stand out as special – those will be the ones you will use as affirmations for the next 21 days.

They say it takes 21 days to establish a new habit. Therefore, your spiritual practice will be to read or recite your new truths every day. You will be feeling, knowing and breathing into your new truths for the next 21 days to firmly establish those new thoughts and feelings.

Don't worry if similar affirmations didn't work in the past. They can now. The soil is fertile. Plant your seeds and water them every day for the next 3 weeks and you will be good to go.

As you have done with each journaling prompt before now, call in your spiritual support, take a self-loving breath, and trust yourself. You now know your previous pattern better than anyone. Bring in the joy as you ask, and answer, the questions only you can now ask and answer.

Your Journaling Prompt:

As you think about all the writing you just completed, and all the energy that has shifted as a result of your effort, what is your honest to goodness truth now? What are you most excited to know and celebrate about yourself now? What have you known all along but couldn't really grasp before? What surprised you the most? What strengths do you have that before you could not appreciate? What deeper understanding do you now have about yourself?

What is the truth about you in the most positive sense? What is the truth about your place in the world and the gift that you are? What stands out to you about the beauty of your own spirit?

As you think about your new life now without this pattern, for what do you feel most grateful? What is most worth celebrating about how you will now be in the world?

What is the truth now about how you will behave? What is the truth about how you will think and feel? What is the truth about what you deserve to experience?

What is the truth about fears that your pattern had caused? What is true now that you will no longer be influenced by the family and cultural messages of your pattern? What is the truth now that you no longer need to compensate for this pattern? What is true in regard to the threats and benefits? What is true about your personality traits?

How many to write? Write as many as you hear, feel and sense. This is what you have been working for – this is how you know you've cleared it.

So, write like the wind.

When all your new truths are finished expressing, go back over them and choose the ones that you really love. Those truths are going to be your affirmations for the next few weeks while you practice feeling these new truths in your body. An affirmation is a positive statement of truth that, at this point, will likely feel more real to you than it ever has before.

Be sure to thank your spiritual guidance for keeping you safe and on track. Give yourself lots of credit for your new expanded awareness. Awesome job! You are officially free of this pattern. You now are free to bask in the glow of this new light that is totally you. It always has been you, except now you can honestly know it. Congratulations!! I'm so happy for you!! And, I'm so grateful to you. You just gave yourself and the world a valuable gift.

Chapter Twenty-Nine:
Noticing What's Different

In the hopeful event you are reading this after having cleared a pattern, congratulations! You just made way for energy to move in a more positive direction in your life and now it is time to notice what is different for you.

In the hours and days following a thorough clearing session, insights will continue to drop into your awareness. Please embrace these new insights because you've earned them. You did the work. You released old energy and brought in new energy. And, you have achieved a new way of being in the world.

Things have shifted for you, and now it is time to notice how your thoughts and experiences have shifted, and to celebrate these changes. It is not only okay to do this, your appreciation of your new insights and behaviors help lock them into their permanent placement.

You may notice the deep introspection required to transform your more complex patterns can leave you feeling open and vulnerable. It's like being a new parent, where your heart opens to receive your newborn child; meanwhile, the harsh realities of the world can feel even harsher in comparison. Therefore, you may wish to make careful choices about how often you engage in this process and you might choose to have professional support while you engage. If you've never had the comfort of professional support, now may be a great time to consider it. It can be powerfully healing and nurturing to have wise counsel to share ideas with and to accompany you on your journey.

It is also important to note that friends and family have grown used to our behaviors the way they were, and have become accustomed to doing a certain emotional dance with us. Therefore, there may be those who, despite your successful inner work, do not notice you are no longer provoked by certain triggers and still try to continue the old emotional dance. To avoid this, I have found it helpful to share my goals for my inner work with those closest to me. I do this not only because I want their support, but also because clearing patterns shifts how we relate to each other and I want to give my dear ones fair notice and invite them to grow with me. It can be scary for loved ones when we change, as they may fear being left behind. One friend actually said to me – *Please don't change too much.*

Regardless of who notices, you can still enjoy the differences you observe in yourself. While it is nice when others notice our efforts to change, and it is encouraging when others choose to grow with us, we do not need the world around us to change in order for us to be in a state of freedom and joy. In fact, that's the whole idea. You can't go wrong with keeping your focus on evolving your own life, and unleashing your own bliss.

You may notice that you observe your thoughts and behaviors in a new light, even as they are happening, because you now have new frameworks for evaluating them. You now have new self-discovery skills and I encourage you to enjoy many more sacred clearing sessions, getting to the *root of the root* of the issues you most want to address. You can now create moments of clarity whenever you need them. Greater peace is possible each time you claim a new intention and work through these Discovery Prompts.

The process in this book is effective, but it is not easy. Some will tell you that you can heal your life without revisiting the past or without extending any real effort. This is simply not true. Any other way that doesn't involve a person looking deeply at the rooting of their false beliefs misses discovering the lessons and gifts of their struggles. There is a gift in every struggle and there is really no more effort in choosing to find the gift than there is in choosing to continue to struggle.

While I have experienced that there are plateaus we can reach, inner-growth and self-discovery is a lifelong journey. In fact, I've noticed that as my skills increase, so do my challenges. I then develop new skills to meet those new challenges, and on and on. Please have faith in yourself to untangle the issues in your life, and keep going even when it appears that life is giving you the same lesson on a different day. It may just be that life is giving you a new challenge to push your skills to the next level. Without the challenge, you might not know that your skills have increased.

I call the peace and freedom I have gained from this practice Lotus Flower Living, but you may call your experience by another name or maybe no name at all. When you transform struggle into strength that strength wants to be directed somewhere. You might choose to go to the next level of inner work or you may wish to help others in some way or channel your new freedom into new creative endeavors, or all of the above.

Those, like you, who venture to do deep inner work, are the true leaders. You are the sensitive, courageous warriors who embrace the inner struggle and use it to grow beyond confusion and bring clarity to your own life and to everyone else whose life you touch.

I hope you choose to change as many patterns from struggle into peace that you can. I hope you choose to awaken the lotus flower within you and find many awakening points beyond. It has been my honor to spend time with you in these pages. My prayer for you is wherever your inner work takes you on your emotional-spiritual journey you feel loved and supported every step of the way.

With gratitude and respect,

Julie Matheson

Appendix

Glossary

Affirmation – Powerful, personal, present tense, 'I' statements declaring a desired condition, as though it already exists, such as – *I deeply and profoundly love myself.*

Affirmative Prayer – Claiming the condition we want to experience as though it already exists. An affirmative prayer is the act of unifying with the co-creative principle of Life, saying many related affirmations together to create a mental-emotional state that causes you to vibrate at the same frequency as the condition you wish to manifest, thereby inviting those circumstances to manifest in your experience.

All Possible – The all-encompassing omnipotent and omnipresent realm that holds an etheric blueprint of anything we might wish to manifest or co-create. The realm in which we are all interconnected. Used in place of the word God to broaden the meaning of the word God in terms of the law of cause and effect.

Archetype – Generic stories and themes that play out across time and across societal contexts and constraints. Archetypes are often the themes of popular books, poems and movies: the hero, the scapegoat, the fool, the invisible child, the bully, the victim, the damsel in distress, and there are countless others.

Body Intelligence – The innate, nature-spirit wisdom of your body.

Body Memory – Information about your past encoded in your cells.

Charge – Heightened, exaggerated or excessive emotional energy associated with a feeling.

Circular Thinking – Negative, energy-draining thoughts that have not been reconciled.

Clearing Work – The practice of removing the energy of a system of dysfunctional thoughts and beliefs, replacing them with higher vibrational, functional thoughts and beliefs.

Co-creation – The act of participating with the creative principle of life to manifest new experiences. Also, commonly referred to as the Law of Attraction or the Law of Cause and Effect.

Co-Creative Energy – The all-encompassing omnipotent and omnipresent power, with which we participate to manifest our experiences. Used in place of the word God to broaden the meaning of the word God in terms of the law of cause and effect.

Emotional Body – The energy that surrounds and permeates your body. Your thoughts and feelings influence the quality, density and vibration of your emotional body. The emotional body influences your physical body.

Energetic Signature – As it relates to the lotus flower signature, it is a vibrational reference point of recognition, an ethereal symbol that some finely tuned intuitive practitioners can actually see.

Energy – The vibration of beliefs, thoughts, feelings, people, places and things.

Filter – The lens you see the world through as influenced by your personality, ego, astrological chart, programmed inner-child and inner-parent dialogue, cultural messages from your community, unique health challenges, past life experiences and many beliefs from years of emotional imprints from every kind of personal experience.

Give-Receive Cycle – A reciprocal energy exchange.

Healing – A healthy shift in perception (or opinion) based on real facts. As it relates to physical illness, this doesn't necessarily mean *cure*.

Inner Child – The child you once were that still lives inside of you, influencing your beliefs, thoughts, feelings, behavior and creativity.

Issue – A problematic condition, experience or circumstance.

Karma – The idea that what we put out into the world through our thoughts, words, actions and beliefs comes back to us reflected in our experiences. It also pertains to unfinished past life themes that affect us in this lifetime. This is a model of thinking that is often used to describe the way energy moves.

Knowing – Unwavering certainty that comes from a place within that is connected to higher awareness.

Law of Cause and Effect – The spiritual principle of Life that makes it possible for beliefs, thoughts and feelings to directly impact our experience.

Life – As used in this book, Oneness, Divine Source, Universal Intelligence, Unlimited Potential, God, Goddess.

Lotus Flower Living Journaling Practice – A step-by-step journaling practice designed to energetically clear out limiting beliefs by making known the pattern of thought-logic central to a particular issue, giving your heart and mind a chance to make new decisions.

Negative Pattern – A set of painful, frustrating beliefs, thoughts and behaviors that have repeated more than once, and which you resist happening again.

Negative Truth – Thoughts, feelings and perceptions of current problematic circumstances.

Pattern – An experience, behavior, thought or automatic response that has happened more than once which you would like to stop.

Perception – Subjective sensory awareness and observation not necessarily based on concrete facts.

Positive Pattern – A sustainable, balanced set of positive beliefs, thoughts and behaviors working together to reinforce a positive perception, which fosters positive experiences.

Root Cause – The original reason for a certain condition.

Soul Contract – Agreements we made with others, at the soul level, before we were born, based on what we most wanted to learn or experience in order to evolve.

Soul-Logic – Irrefutable intelligence drawing from a broad spectrum of wisdom. The wisdom that comes from one's soul that is connected to Divinity.

True Reality – Unlimited potential in its purest essence: beauty, wisdom, intelligence, health, abundance, creativity, integrity, balance, ease, grace and joy.

True Unlimited Potential – The all-encompassing omnipotent and omnipresent power within and around us with which we participate to manifest our experiences according to our deeply held beliefs. Used in place of the word God to broaden the meaning of the word God in terms of the law of cause and effect.

Discovery Prompt Quick Reference Guide

Discovery Prompt 1: State the Issue

The most painful issue is the highest priority issue to address first. Feel the issue in your body and let it tell you what bothers you about it. What happens when the pattern is activated? Describe, the best you can, the issue just as you sense it. Stay present and remember to breathe.

Discovery Prompt 2: Set Your Highest Intention

Acknowledge that a solution exists. Imagine how you want to feel once your issue is resolved. What would life feel like without this issue? How would life be better for you? Claim your intention for your clearing work. My life without this pattern will look and feel like_____. I claim this or something better.

Discovery Prompt 3: Identify Your Pattern's Limiting Beliefs

What is your pattern's most negative truth? List your pattern's lies, messages, limiting beliefs, truths, half-truths, full truths, distorted facts, real facts – anything and everything negative about your pattern. For example – *It tells me I am _____ (stupid, ineffective, worthless, etc.). I feel _____ about this issue.* Write as fast as you can all the limiting thoughts and beliefs just as you hear them in exactly the same way the pattern speaks to you.

Discovery Prompt 4: Seek Out Your Pattern's Hiding Strategies

What strategies does your pattern use to confuse or distract you from the larger issue? List as many hiding strategies as you can think of, as they relate to your pattern. Name the ways your pattern causes you to avoid, compensate, cope or distract you from the real issue. Feel free to list more as you think of them.

Discovery Prompt 5: Voice Your Family Messages

At the level of your pattern, the family messages you received in childhood influence the ways you think about yourself and your life. As you think of your pattern, identify the limiting beliefs you may have received from your family, such as the ways you behaved in childhood to feel safe, to belong or to get approval. In regard to my issue, my family tells me _____. Be sure to trust your body awareness. Expect to be surprised by what you discover.

Discovery Prompt 6: Consider Your Cultural Messages

Cultural thinking can often be made up of shared, limited, biased and prejudiced opinions that patterns use to trick us into believing the way we believe is normal and right. As you think about your pattern, in terms of your sense of belonging, what thoughts do you hear, feel or sense that distort and confuse your true, grounded, practical and spiritual sense of what is right for you? Ask yourself: In regard to my issue, my culture tells me_____.

Discovery Prompt 7: Acknowledge How Your Pattern Affects Your Body

Here you acknowledge how your beloved body has been compensating for, and has been affected by, your thoughts and actions. Name your physical conditions, as many as you can think of, to fully honor your body. If you've experienced a physical condition and feel it might be related to your pattern, or even if you aren't sure, write it down. Your body thanks you for listening to it.

Discovery Prompt 8: Recognize Your Habits, Obsessions and Compulsions

Name your pattern's habits, obsessions and compulsions by answering the following questions:

When I am sad, my pattern tells me I will feel better by doing _____.

When my feelings are hurt, the first thing I do is _____.

After a long day at work when I feel depleted, I _____.

When I feel jealous my tendency is to _____.

My pattern causes me to use other people to feel better by _____.

I absolutely cannot stop doing _____.

When I am angry, lonely, tired or hungry, I tend to _____.

People say I _____ too much.

I avoid certain tasks or I procrastinate by _____.

Discovery Prompt 9: Give Voice to Your Traumas, Shame, Phobias and Fear

With your Highest Intention in mind, feel your current issue in your body and using your list-prompts from previous steps, think back to when you've felt this way before. Revisit past scenes just enough to get the messages that got encoded. Try to identify your pattern's emotionally shocking and traumatic themes noting each specific event per theme – starting with the earliest event you can recall to the most recent – including acknowledging the emotions and decisions you may have made as a result of each theme. Be sure to note associated phobias, core fear and core shame.

Discovery Prompt 10: Explore Your Past (Lives) and Karma

If you know your past life story that relates to your pattern, go ahead and jot it down. Evaluate it and see how it relates to your pattern. Note the general theme and the corresponding, supporting beliefs. If you do not know your past life themes but are open to the possibility of your pattern being rooted in a past lifetime, simply let yourself wonder about it. Another option is to identify your pattern's archetypal story. For example, is it a *Cinderella* theme, a *betrayal* theme, a *being made the fool* theme, a *self-sabotage* theme, a *power and control* theme? All we are trying to do here is to pop you out of a story by identifying the story you are in.

Discovery Prompt 11: Shed Light on Your Pattern's Resentments, Self-Sabotaging Tendencies and Prideful Opinions

With lightness of heart, and knowing these are nothing more than predictable, common pattern strategies, give yourself the relief of admitting any resentments, hatreds, grudges or feelings of jealousy that may be hidden in your pattern. Further identify how your pattern's resentments cause you to sabotage your own best efforts. What do you value and how does your pattern cause you to behave contrary to those values? How or what does your pattern cause you to misperceive? What are your strong prideful opinions and arrogances in regard to your pattern? What are your exaggerated strengths? What, if anything, does your pattern tell you to help you feel superior to others or above it all?

Discovery Prompt 12: Reveal Your Pattern's Threats and Intimidation

Every pattern has within it a bully, a threatening voice, which tries to prevent you from evolving beyond its influence. Here we identify the specific threats it makes. What frightening things does your pattern say will happen if you let it go? Note where you feel these threats in your body, remember to breathe, and do write them down noticing the contrast between the threat itself and what the threat is actually delivering. Stay focused on the central fears and concerns of your pattern as you list these messages.

Discovery Prompt 13: Expose Your Pattern's False Benefits

Every pattern has within it a convincing voice saying your current way of thinking is benefitting you. This voice says – *Do not change this pattern because if you do, you will lose important assets.* Identify your pattern's benefits and advantages, noticing the falsity of its claims. If you can get more, that's great but at least try to name as many benefits as you listed for threats. You may find naming benefits helps you think of more threats. Be sure to notice where you feel these messages in your body and do write them down. Notice the difference between what your pattern promises versus your actual experience.

Discovery Prompt 14: Untangle Your Pattern's Indecision Loops

Indecision messages in patterns cause the biggest energy drain of all. This pattern aspect presents itself as an impossible dilemma, and, can feel like an unsolvable puzzle where you feel truly stuck. You will hear thoughts about choices you feel you absolutely have to sort out but can't because the choices are layered with complications your mind can't reconcile. You might try finishing the following statements – When it comes to my issue –

I am most perplexed by _____,

I can't reconcile _____.

I go back and forth in an endless state of indecision about _____.

Discovery Prompt 15: Clear the Energy

Read, breathe deeply and feel the truth of these statements:

I now allow any and all lingering traces of negative energy associated with this issue to be fully and completely released, knowing I get to keep what was good and am only releasing that which no longer serves me.

I now fully and completely release all the limiting beliefs of this pattern.

I now fully and completely release the family and cultural messages that no longer serve me in regard to this issue.

I forgive myself and everyone else who contributed to this issue. We are all free.

I thank my body wisdom for its assistance with this work and I am grateful for all it has done to help me compensate for these limiting messages. I now claim all associated physical conditions are harmonized and/or completely healed. My body is free of this entire pattern, and so am I.

I fully accept all gifts gained from the addictions of this pattern and I now fully and completely harmonize, upgrade, integrate and/or release as appropriate all addictions. I forgive all of it.

I fully accept all gifts gained from my past traumatic circumstances and I now fully and completely harmonize, upgrade, integrate and release all negative energy associated with those circumstances from this, and past lives.

I am now free of the energy of any grievances, self-sabotaging habits and exaggerated prideful opinions in regard to this issue.

I now claim that all personality traits and compensating strategies are upgraded and harmonized.

I refute and release all supposed benefits and advantages this pattern falsely promised me.

I refute and release all threats and intimidation this pattern falsely used to frighten me.

I now fully release the double binds, indecision loops and supposed dilemmas of this pattern, and gratefully accept all the wisdom I derived from them. My life is now greatly improved by my own effort. Tomorrow when I wake up, and after my mind and heart have had a chance to reconfigure themselves, my life will be different and better. I feel it, I believe it and I know it. And, so it is....

Discovery Prompt 16: Declare Your New Truth

With each and every step you have been clearing out the old energy and incrementally bringing in new light and energy. Here you will fully call in that light, energy and information by naming it. Your mind and heart need to know exactly how your perception has shifted in order to fully appreciate that it has actually shifted. So, in this final step we acknowledge our new awareness about our newly cleared issue. Referring back to your originally stated issue, ask a question that is aimed directly at the original issue. Write as many truths as you can.

My honest to goodness truth now is _____.

The Truth is all is well.

The Truth is I am always loved.

The Truth is I am always safe.

The Truth is I am lovable and worthy.

The Truth is there is nothing to fear.

The Truth is it is possible to shift my perception.

The truth is there is a deeper reason for everything and now that I know how to discover the deeper truth of what motivates me, I can create whatever I wish from a place of Love and Balance.

That's the Truth.

Acknowledgments

Jim Matheson, my husband and longtime personal in-house editor. You soften the way I write, and you never seem as busy as you always are whenever I ask you to read my writing. That's because 'I'm Primary,' and Primary people always come first.

Patricia Young, my mom, who died in 2014 and who is still with me in spirit. A natural editor and wordsmith, I am grateful to have had you as an early reader and advocate of this work. You read my writing to me with such a loving voice I couldn't help but hear it that way, too.

Kimberly Heim, Michelle Hanafee and Liz Davis-Chaffin. Thank you for keeping me grounded, real and loved through this entire process. Your love and friendship are so dear to me it brings me to tears just writing this.

Stuart Horwitz, BookArchitecture.com. Thank you for appreciating the purpose of this book, for holding my vision while you so gently and expertly coached this material out of me, and for making sure every sentence, paragraph and chapter are in the right order. And, bravely, you were the first to 'test' the writing prompts. Without your loving guidance and amazingly intuitive writing methods, this book would not exist.

Susan Hagen, SusanHagen.com. Thank you for overseeing the final draft of the discovery prompts. Our recorded sessions could be offered as an audiobook for writers. Your ability to reflect back in real time with such accurate detail what I've read to you over the phone still amazes me.

C. Susan Nunn, of CSusanNunn.com. Thank you for your enthusiasm, expertise and care with this spiritual material. You have gone above and beyond to preserve my natural writing voice and have made the final editing stages warm and fun.

James Krause, PixelFlyCreative.com. I was writing at a coffee shop, toying with how to do the graphics for an article, and I "hear" clear as day, "Why don't you ask the person beside you?" Turns out you had written 17 books on graphic design. Thanks, James, for your expertise for the cover design, author photo and my lotus flower drawing in the text.

A special thank you to the following practitioners, who each encouraged, counseled, inspired, and validated both my personal healing process and/or the contents of this book. I deeply appreciate your brave, pure hearts:

Judith Swack, Ph.D. Thank you profoundly for showing me it is possible to clear a pattern in one session. Although I may present them differently, most of the Discovery Prompts in this book were inspired and informed by your teaching. I am deeply grateful to you for being an innovative teacher and guide, a true spiritual leader and champion of the human spirit.

Linda Squires, D.C. I am grateful for your dedication and wisdom while we explored so many spiritual concepts together. I don't know what I would have done without your clarity, integrity and gentleness all those years I faced my own patterning. And, of course, so much gratitude to you for recognizing the lotus flower, knowing what it all meant and for having the fortitude to relay that information to me.

Robin Wiseman, Intuitive Healer. I can always count on every session with you to bring forth some kind of surprising miracle. I appreciate your keen ability to relay such accurate and resonating information, and for validating the lotus flower energy countless times, while I figured out what it all meant.

Emmy Morgan, Intuitive Healer. Your purity of spirit and integrity always lead the way, whether you are advising me about this book or my life.

Juelle Wilkins, of Blue Star of Hope. Thank you for loaning me your phrase *I love you and yes*, and for your ongoing friendship, love and support. Your Power of One Programs inspire me to greater service. I started writing this book soon after our service trip with you and Donovan to Thailand.

Greta Bro, Expressive Therapist. Thanks to you, I wrote this book with my reader's inner child consistently in my mind.

Debra Byer, D.C., Licac. Thank you, Debra, for your unwavering, loving support of my mind, body and spirit. You are a true friend and healer.

Mike Levesque, of Timing Edge Astrology. Thanks, Mike, for seeing a writer in my astrological chart and for so consistently saying to me, "Write the book!"

Kim DeWit and Lisa Compton. Thank you for being my Boise, Idaho spiritual support team.

Thank you to the following book companions for being readers and/or editors, encouragers/educators: Pam Niland, Debbie Dalrymple, Randa Vatric, Ned Avidson, Sofia Dorsano, Caitlin Firestone, Andrea Fox, Eva Williams, Christine Ball and Mary Ann Matheson.

Chloe Marsala, Copy-Editor. Such care and expertise went into your efforts to help shape the initial stage of this book. You have an admirable ability to find just the right word.

Francis Woods, Editor/Writer. I appreciate your gentle spirit and our serendipitous meeting. Thank you for your keen eyes after mine were worn out and missing things.

Hillary Rettig. I often reference in my mind and heart what I learned in your thoughtful, potent class at Grub Street, *How To Write A Lot*.

And finally, my sincere appreciation to my spiritual counterparts at the Centers for Spiritual Living: CSL Reno, NV; CSL Greater Boston, MA and CSL Columbus, Ohio.

Suggested Reading List and Courses

Bach, Richard. <u>Jonathan Livingston Seagull</u>

Beatty, Melody. <u>CoDependent No More</u>

Beaucaire, Michal; Artwork Provided by Heussenstamm, Paul. <u>The Art of Mandala Meditation: Mandala Designs to Heal Your Mind, Body and Spirit</u>

Beckwith, Michael Bernard. <u>Life Visioning: A Transformative Process of Activating Your Unique Gifts and Highest Potential</u>

Daniel, Alma; Wyllie, Timothy. <u>Ask Your Angels: A Practical Guide to Working with the Messengers of Heaven to Empower and Enrich Your Life</u>

Dyer, Wayne, Dr. <u>Change Your Thoughts – Change Your Life: Living the Wisdom of the Tao</u>

Dyer, Wayne, Dr. <u>The Power of Intention</u>

Eden, Donna. <u>Energy Medicine: Balancing Your Body's Energies for Optimal Health, Joy, and Vitality</u>

Hay, Louise. <u>You Can Heal Your Life</u>

Holmes, Ernest. <u>Creative Mind and Success</u>

Holmes, Ernest. <u>The Science of Mind</u>

Holmes, Ernest. <u>The Thing Called You</u>

Maitri, Sandra. <u>The Spiritual Dimension of the Enneagram: Nine Faces of the Soul</u>

McCann, Eileen; Shannon, Douglas. <u>The Two Step: The Dance Towards Intimacy</u>

Myss, Carolyn. <u>Anatomy of the Spirit: The Seven Stages of Power and Healing</u>

Myss, Carolyn. <u>Sacred Contracts: Awakening Your Divine Potential</u>

Nepo, Mark. <u>Finding Inner Courage</u>

Rasha. <u>Oneness.</u>

Riso, Don Richard; Hudson, Russ. <u>The Wisdom of the Enneagram: The Complete Guide to Psychological and Spiritual Growth for the Nine Personality Types</u>

Schultz, Mona Lisa, M.D. Ph.D. <u>Awakening Intuition: Using Your Mind-Body Network for Insight and Healing</u>

Taylor, Terry Lynn; Crain, Mary Beth. <u>Angel Wisdom: 365 Meditations and Insights From the Heavens</u>

Tolle, Eckhart. <u>The Power of Now</u>

Troward, Thomas. <u>The Edinburgh and Dore Lectures on Mental Science</u>

Wagele, Elizabeth; Baron, Renee. <u>The Enneagram Made Easy: Discover the Nine Types of People</u>

Walsch, Neale Donald. <u>Conversations with God</u>

Weiss, Brian L. <u>Many Lives Many Masters</u>

William, Anthony. <u>Medical Medium Life-Changing Foods</u>

Wright, Machaelle Small. <u>MAP: The Co-Creative White Brotherhood Medical Assistance Program</u> (Please do not be offended by the name – *white* refers to all the spectrums and vibrations of light and *brotherhood* refers to the family of all life.)

Yee, Colleen Saidman. <u>Yoga for Life: A Journey to Inner Peace and Freedom</u>

Audio Courses and Recordings

Choquette, Sonia. True Balance: A Commonsense Guide to Renewing Your Spirit

Packer, Duane. Roman, Sanaya. Awakening Your Light Body (six-part course series) – DaBen Meditations (Packer) and Orin Meditations (Roman) www.orindaben.com

Palmer, Helen. Sounds True. The Enneagram

Roman, Sanaya. Packer, Duane. <u>Opening to Channel: How to Connect With Your Guide</u>

Roman, Sanaya. Transcending Your Ego (six-part course series) – Orin Meditations

Roman, Sanaya. Transforming with Divine Will – Orin Meditations www.orindaben.com

www.orindaben.com

Tolle, Eckhart. Living the Liberated Life and Dealing with the Pain-Body

Movies for Your Inner Child

The Kid. Directed by Jon Turteltaub. Performances by Bruce Willis, Emily Mortimer, Spencer Breslin, Lily Tomlin and Jean Smart. Walt Disney Pictures, 2000.

Inside Out. Directed by Pete Docter. Performances by Amy Poehler, Phyllis Smith, Richard Kind, Lewis Black, Bill Hader and Mindy Kaling. Pixar Production Studios, 2015.

Programs Available Worldwide

Centers for Spiritual Living: Core spiritual education classes, practitioner classes and ministerial coursework

Landmark Forum Education Workshops and Classes

12 Step Programs, especially Al-Anon and CoDA

Receive a FREE Journal

You may download a free copy of
The Lotus Flower Living Companion Journal (.pdf) at
LotusFlowerLiving.com/Book
by validating the purchase of this book.

About Julie

Hi there – I'm Jim Matheson, or as I am known in spiritual circles, Julie's husband. Julie felt her bio ought to be written by someone other than herself, and so I am honored to share this nontraditional 'About the Author' page.

Julie is a metaphysician, studying the deepest roots of thought, consciousness and co-creation. Her work is the manifestation of her life's journey, so it is ever evolving and deepening. Julie earned her undergraduate degree in Human Ecology at The Ohio State University and, after the last of several moves as a Navy wife brought her to Boston, she earned her Master's in Psychology and Expressive Therapies at Lesley University in Cambridge, MA.

Along the way, Julie has dedicated countless hours to her holistic counseling training and myriad other programs and retreats, all with the singular goal of understanding how the universe really works and applying this knowledge to take responsibility for her own life and growth. Julie launched her private holistic counseling practice in 1999 with the 'soul' mission of helping others along their journey of self-discovery. Most impressive to me is that I have watched Julie fill countless stacks of yellow legal pads with her journaling and pattern clearing work, which ultimately informs how she teaches this process.

Julie loves healthy food, to sit quietly with a cup of tea, and take long walks. She (and I) enjoy visiting new places, which usually entails a trip to the local health food and metaphysical book stores to take in their energy and learn what is happening by perusing the community bulletin boards.

Many years ago, we agreed to always have fresh flowers in our home as their beauty and wisdom help bring us closer to heaven on earth. Julie's work, and this book, is meant to do the very same thing in a deep and lasting way.

You can learn more about Julie and her work at: www.lotusflowerliving.com

Ingram Content Group UK Ltd.
Milton Keynes UK
UKHW052259250623
424008UK00029B/382

9 781733 780780